Year 2
Workbook

Pearson

Published by Pearson Education Limited, 80 Strand, London, WC2R 0RL.
www.pearson.com/international-schools

Copies of official specifications for all Pearson Edexcel qualifications may be found on the website:
https://qualifications.pearson.com

Text © Pearson Education Limited 2023
Produced by Just Content Ltd
Designed by PDQ Media Digital Media Solutions
Typeset by PDQ Media Digital Media Solutions
Picture research by Straive Ltd
Original illustrations © Pearson Education Limited 2023
Cover design © Pearson Education Limited 2023

The right of Lesley Butcher to be identified as the author of this work has been asserted by her in
accordance with the Copyright, Designs and Patents Act 1988.

First published 2023

26 25
11

British Library Cataloguing in Publication Data
A catalogue record for this book is available from the British Library

ISBN 978 1 292 43329 5

Printed in the UK by Bell & Bain

Contents

Health and growth

Humans need food to grow. The correct amount of food and water keeps humans alive. There are many ways we can help ourselves to stay healthy.

In this topic we will learn:

- that humans need the correct amounts of food and water
- that there are many types of food and diets
- about the main food groups
- that a balanced diet contains the correct amount of all the main food groups
- that we need to exercise to stay healthy
- that human and animal babies need different parental care
- that personal hygiene and food hygiene are important for health
- why humans take medicines.

Choose two key words from the box above.
Write or draw what they mean.

Food and water

1 a) Complete the sentences using the words in the box. Use each word once.

> regularly   amounts   exercise   cool   healthy

Humans need food and water in the correct

_______________ to stay _______________.

Humans sweat when they are hot and when

they _______________. Sweat helps to

_______________ our bodies.

We need to drink water _______________.

b) Which life process is each of these?

eating food _______________

exercising _______________

2 These are drinking bottles for water.

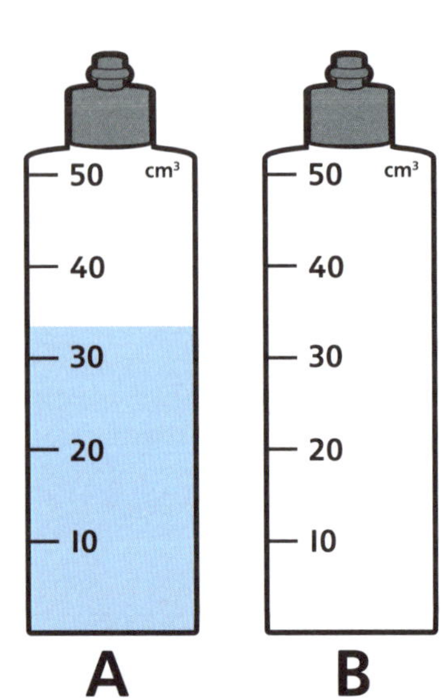

a)   How much water is in bottle **A**? _____ cm³

b)   Draw 40 cm³ of water in bottle **B**.

3) Ahmed records how many glasses of water he drinks every day for 5 days.

Day	Number of glasses of water	Totals
Monday		2
Tuesday	卌	
Wednesday	IIII	
Thursday		6
Friday	III	

a)   Draw the missing tallies and complete the totals.

b)   On which day did he drink the most water?

____

Balanced diet

1 What does a balanced diet mean?

____

____

2 Draw **two** different meals that you like to eat. Label the foods.

Meal 1

Meal 2

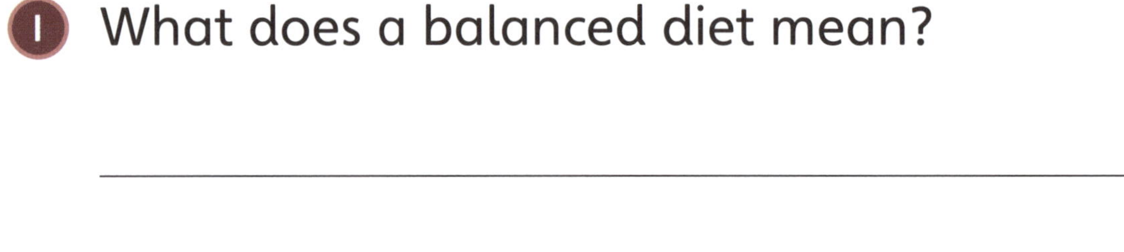

3 A shop has these pictures on food to show which foods are free from certain things.

MEAT FREE DAIRY FREE EGG FREE NUT FREE

What are each of these foods free from?

A 

____

____

B 

____

____

C 

____

____

D 

____

____

Sugary food

1. Circle the picture showing sugary food.

| bread | butter | biscuit | egg |

2. Circle the drink that humans need every day.

| cola | lemonade | milkshake | water |

3. Why do we put sugar in food?

____

4. a) Which living things does sugar come from?

____

   b) What do these living things use to

   make sugar? _____________________

   c) What sugary food do bees make?

   ____

5 Complete this poster to tell people not to eat too much sugary food.
Add words and pictures before you colour.

Starchy food

1 Circle **two** starchy foods.

bread	chocolate	ice lolly	mango	pasta

2 Circle **three** plants that give us starchy food.

rice   strawberry   sweet potato

wheat   potato   apple

3 Name **three** things that we can make with flour.

1. _______________________

2. _______________________

3. _______________________

4 What do starchy foods slowly give our body?

____

5 These shelves are in a shop near where you live. The shop sells **starchy** food.

Draw food on the shelves in packets. Write on the packets to show what is in them.

Protein

1 Circle **two** foods that contain a lot of protein.

cabbage	cheese	cake	fish	melon

2 a) Circle foods that people who have a vegetarian diet do **not** eat.

oranges   meat   bananas   water

ice cream   biscuits   chicken   cream

b) Name **four** foods that contain a lot of **protein** that a person who has a vegetarian diet could eat.

1. __________________________

2. __________________________

3. __________________________

4. __________________________

3 Grace looks at some eggs that have been cooked for different lengths of time.

Time cooked in minutes

| 0 | 1 | 2 | 3 | 5 |

A   B   C   D   E

a) For how long has egg D been cooked?

☐ minutes

b) Which egg has **not** been cooked? __________

c) Describe **one** difference you can see between egg B and egg E.

____

d) Predict what an egg cooked for 4 minutes looks like. Draw a picture.

Fats and dairy foods

1 Name **two** different oils that humans eat.

1. ________________________   2. ________________________

2 a)   Circle all the **dairy** foods.

b)   Name **two starchy** foods in the pictures above.

1. ________________________   2. ________________________

3 a) Complete the sentence.

A lot of milk comes from ___________________

but some comes from ___________________.

b) Adi asks some people which of these four types of milk they like best.

5 people   3 people   8 people   4 people

(i) Complete the tally chart for Adi's results.

Type of milk	Tally	Totals

(ii) Which milk did **most** people like best?

____

(iii) How many people did Adi ask about milk?

Fruits and vegetables

1 Draw lines to match each food with the best description.

olive oil 	fruit
pineapple 	fat
beans 	sugary
pasta 	oil
butter 	starchy
jam biscuit 	protein

2 a) Where do fruits and vegetables come from?

____

b) Fruits give us vitamins.
What else do fruits give us?

____

c) Write **one** way that vitamins help our bodies.

____

d) Name **one** fruit or vegetable that is each of these colours:

green ___________________

yellow ___________________

red ___________________

orange ___________________

purple ___________________

Types of exercise

① Caleb plays football every day.

What does this help him to do?

Tick (✓) **one** box.

☐ eat more vegetables ☐ see things better

☐ exercise regularly ☐ have a balanced diet

② Draw lines to match the people with the activities.

cycling

dancing

jumping

skipping

3 This girl does an activity.

   a) Do you think she does
      the activity **competitively** or for **fun**?

   ____

   b) Give a reason for your choice.

   ____

4 What sort of exercise do you do?

Draw yourself doing some activities.

What happens when we exercise?

1. Draw a line from each picture to show whether the person is breathing in or breathing out.

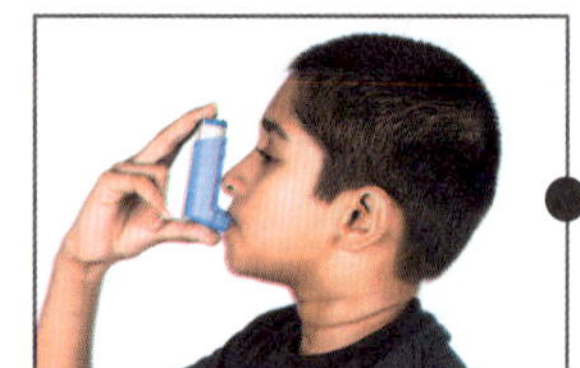

2. Put your hand flat on your chest like this. Breathe normally. Describe what your chest does as you breathe.

____

____

3 Five children exercise. They each count their number of breaths per minute as soon as they stop exercising.

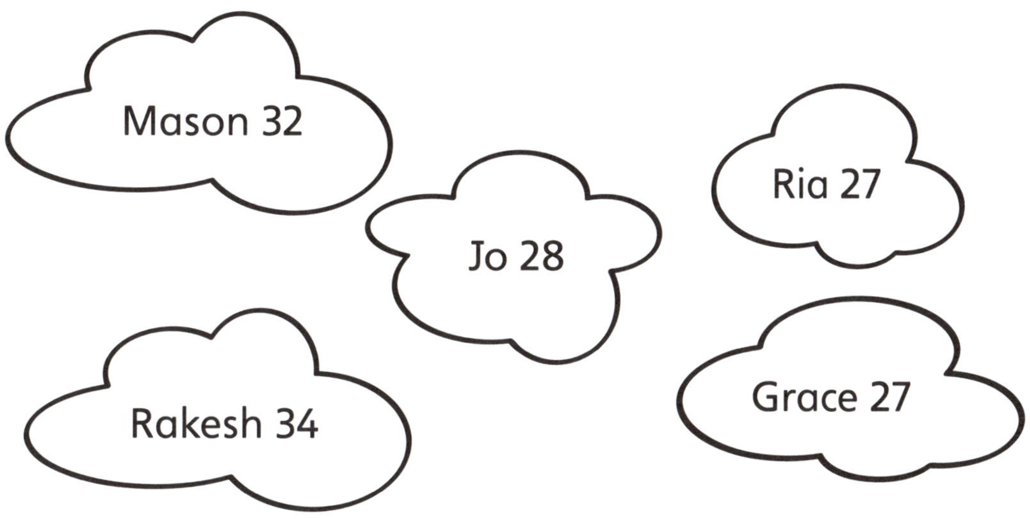

Draw a table to show their results.
Try to use a ruler if you can.

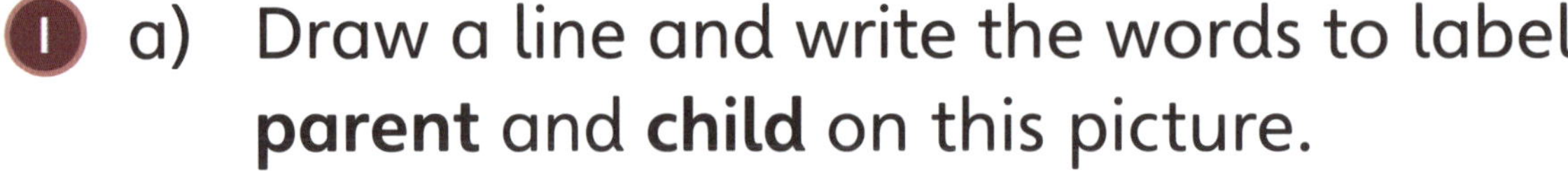

1 a) Draw a line and write the words to label **parent** and **child** on this picture.

b) What does **parental care** mean?

____

c) Why does the baby need parental care?

____

2 This mother takes her baby for a walk. Why does she need to **carry** the baby?

____

3 This father is feeding his baby. What food is he giving the baby?

____

4 What parental care is this parent giving?
One has been done for you.

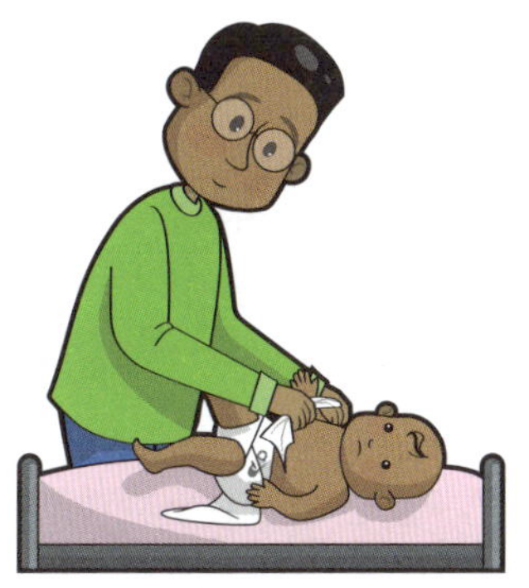  

changing
a nappy   ________________   ________________

                   ________________   ________________

5 Adults show children how to do things.
Draw things that adults showed you how to do.

Parental care in animals

1 Circle the parent animal that gives its babies the most care.

2 The picture shows an adult bird and its three babies.

  a) What do adult birds make for the babies to live in?

  ____

  b) What is the adult bird in the picture doing?

  ____

  c) Describe what the babies' mouths look like.

  ____

  ____

  d) Write **one** thing that baby birds learn to do.

  ____

3 a) How do adult crocodiles help their babies?

b) How do adult kangaroos help their babies?

4 A human is helping this baby hedgehog to stay alive.

Hedgehogs are mammals.

a) What is the human giving to the baby hedgehog?

b) Who usually looks after a baby hedgehog?

c) Baby hedgehogs cannot see when they are born. What can you see in the picture that shows this?

Keeping clean

1 Circle **two** ways to keep teeth healthy.

 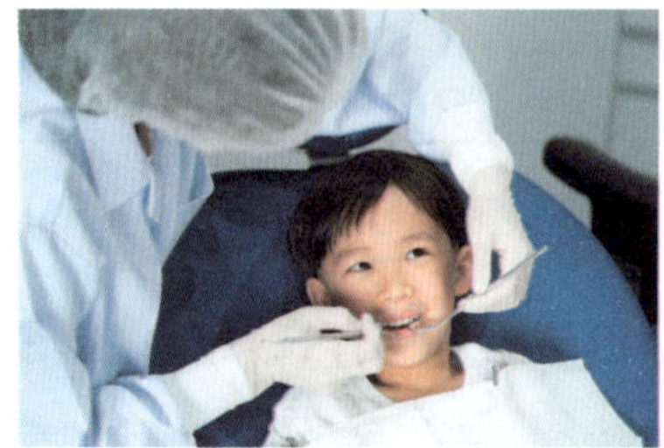 

2 a) What has Miko found in his hair?

____

b) What can Miko's parents do to help remove them?

____

____

3 What are these children doing to keep clean?

4 a) When do you wash your hands?

b) When do you wash your face?

c) We need water to wash. What else do we need?

Safe food to eat

1. Joel washes his hands. 

   a) Why does Joel do this?

   ____

   b) What does he use to wash his hands?

   __________________ and __________________

   c) Seb washed his hands too.

   Why did Seb wash his hands?

   ____

2. This food is unsafe to eat.

   What could happen to someone if they eat this food? 

   ____

3 Circle the **oldest** piece of bread.

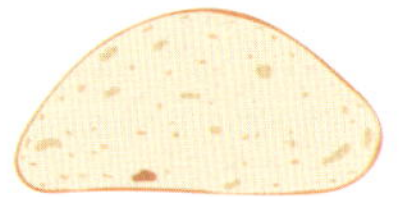   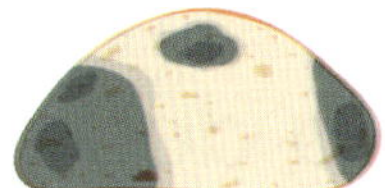

4 This person's job is making cakes.

a) Write **four** things she is wearing to keep the cakes clean.

1. ___________________________________

2. ___________________________________

3. ___________________________________

4. ___________________________________

b) Mrs Najaar buys some cakes.

Why does she put a net over the cakes?

____

____

Feeling unwell

1 a) Circle the child who is dressed up as a doctor.

b) What can a doctor prescribe?

____

c) Why do people go to see a doctor?

____

d) Have you ever been to see a doctor?

Draw what your doctor was like.

2 a) What is this doctor doing?

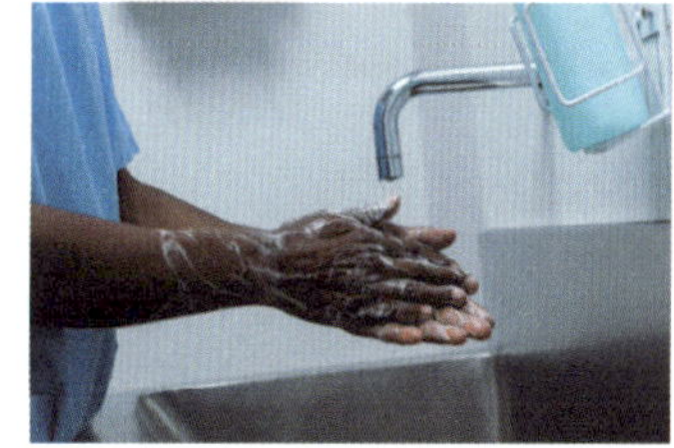

____

b) What **two** things is he using to do this?

_____________________ and _____________________

3 We use this to find out
how hot someone is.

What is this equipment called?

____

4 This doctor does operations on people
who are very unwell.

She wears this equipment.

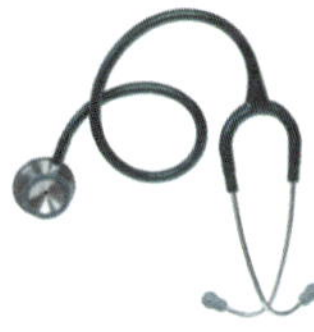

a) Circle the part she puts
into her ears.

b) What does she use this equipment to do?

____

Medicines

1 a) When do humans take medicine?

____

b) What sort of medicine are these? 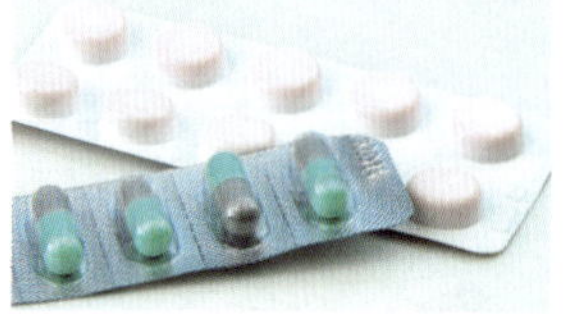

____

c) Who prescribes medicine? ___________________

d) What could happen if someone takes the wrong medicine?

____

2 This cupboard has medicine in it. 

a) Draw a lock on the cupboard.

b) Why is the cupboard door kept locked?

____

3 Why do medicine bottles have special lids? 

____

____

4 Finish the poster to tell people about how to be safe with medicines.

Add words and pictures of your own before colouring.

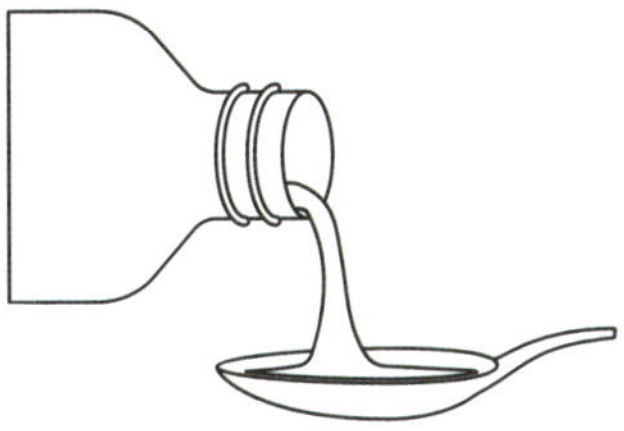

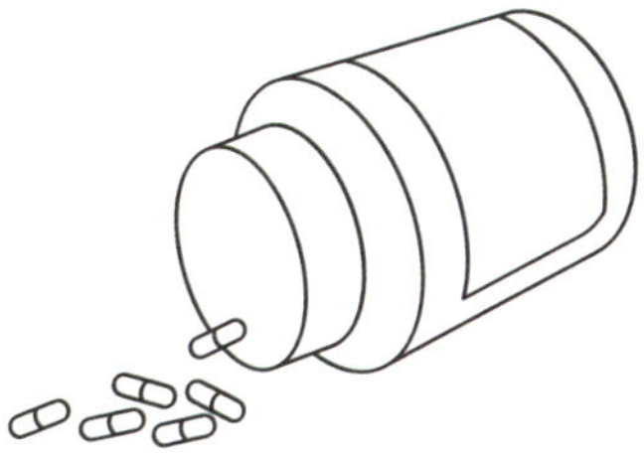

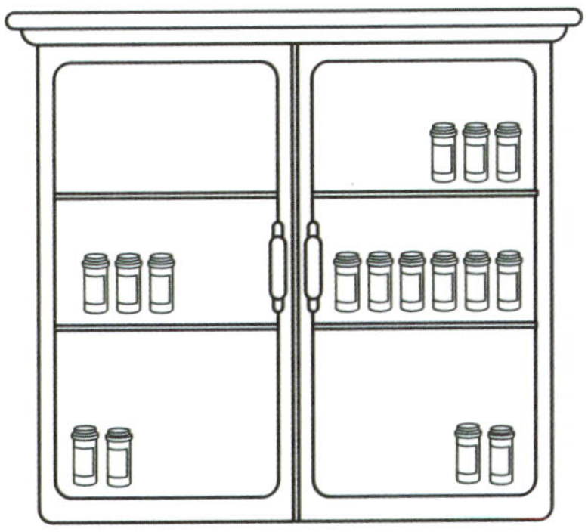

What have I learned?

1. I know that humans need the correct amounts

   of _________________ and _________________ to

   stay alive.

2. I understand that there are many types of food
   and humans may have different diets.

   I know that people with a vegetarian diet do

   not eat _________________.

3. I know that a balanced diet is a diet that

   contains the _________________ amount of all

   the _________________ food _________________.

4. I know the main food groups and can group
   foods correctly. They are:

   sugary and s_________________ foods

   p_________________

   fats and d_________________ food

   f_________________ and v_________________

5 I understand that we need exercise to stay

_______________ .

6 I understand that human and animal babies need different types and amounts of parental care.

I know **two** things that human babies need their parents to do for them.

I. _______________   2. _______________

7 I understand that personal and food hygiene are important for health.

I know **two** ways of keeping myself clean.

I. _______________   2. _______________

I know **two** ways of keeping food safe to eat.

I. _______________   2. _______________

8 I understand why humans take medicines and I know that medicines should be stored away

from _______________ . They should be locked

in a _______________ .

Living things in the environment

Animals and plants must survive in the places where they live. Only the living things that are suited to their environment will survive.

In this topic we will learn:

- that a habitat is a place where animals and plants live
- that within a habitat there may be smaller microhabitats
- to observe features of living things that suit them to a particular habitat
- to suggest how these adaptations help them to survive
- that environmental factors may affect where animals and plants live.

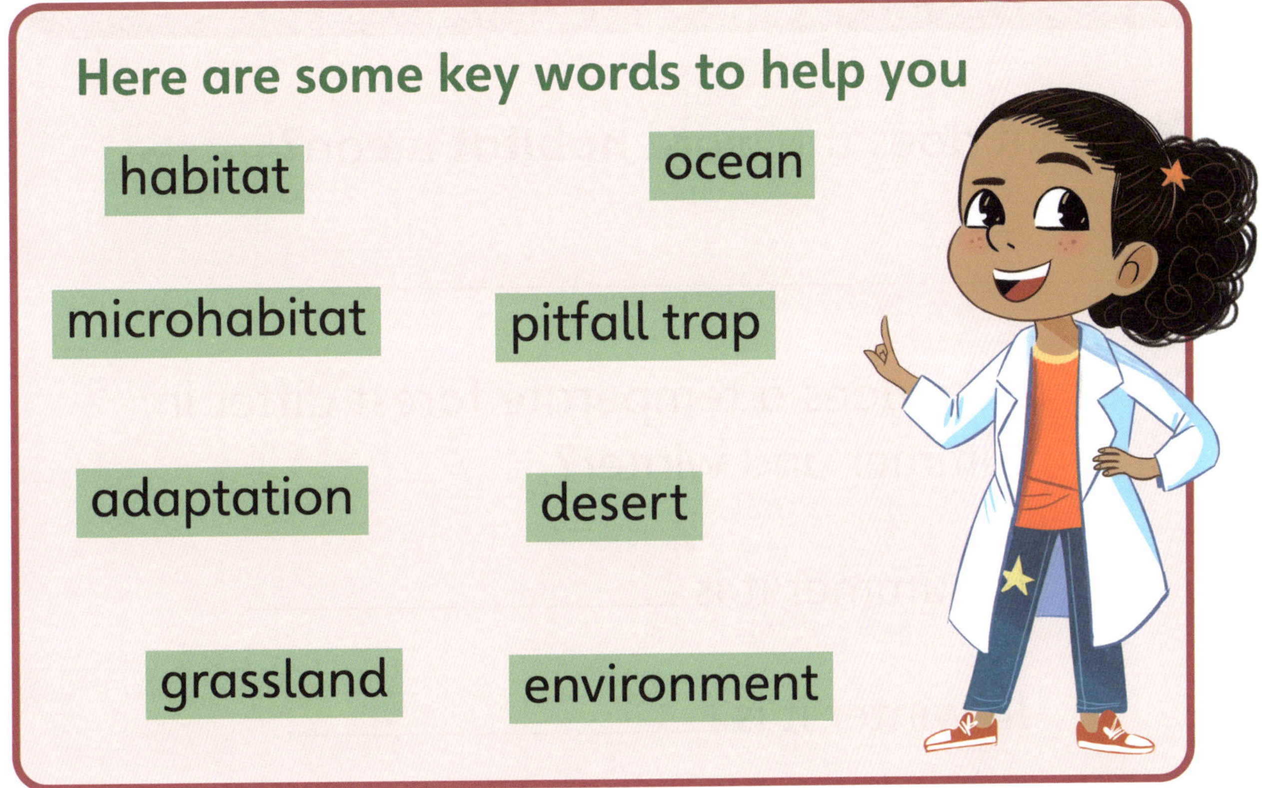

Choose two key words from the box above.
Write or draw what they mean.

Animals in forests

1. What does the word **habitat** mean?

____

2. a) How does a temperate forest differ in summer and winter?

   In summer it is _____________________.

   In winter it is _____________________.

   b) Describe what a **forest** looks like.

   ____

   ____

   c) Describe **two** things that animals can do to survive cold weather.

   1. ____

   2. ____

3. a) Circle **two** words that describe a rainforest.

   warm   dry   cold   wet   snowy

b)   Draw some animals that live in rainforests.
     Write their names.

Animals in water

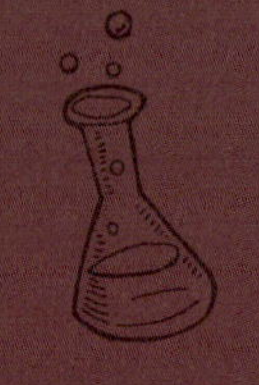

1 a) Tick (✓) which of these covers more of the Earth.

☐ land ☐ ocean

b) What are smaller parts of oceans called?

____

c) What is the water like in an ocean habitat?

____

2 a) A pond is a freshwater habitat.

Write **three more** freshwater habitats.

1. ____pond____   2. ______________

3. ______________   4. ______________

b) How does freshwater differ from ocean water?

____

3 Draw some animals that live in a pond and some that live in an ocean.
Write their names.

4 a)   What are plankton?

____

____

b)   Name an animal that eats plankton.

____

Grassland and desert habitats

1. The picture shows a **grassland** or **savanna** habitat.

Draw some animals living there.
Think about what they are doing.
Will some lie in the shade?
Will some need to drink?

2. Complete the sentences about this habitat.

A grassland habitat is not as dry as a

_______________ habitat but it does not have as

much rainfall as a _______________ habitat.

3 The pictures show desert habitats in the day and at night.

a) Write **day** or **night** under each picture.

__________________ __________________

b) Write some sentences of your own about what it is like in a desert habitat. Use words from the box to help.

dry	rain	hot
night	cooler	animals

____

____

____

____

____

____

Microhabitats

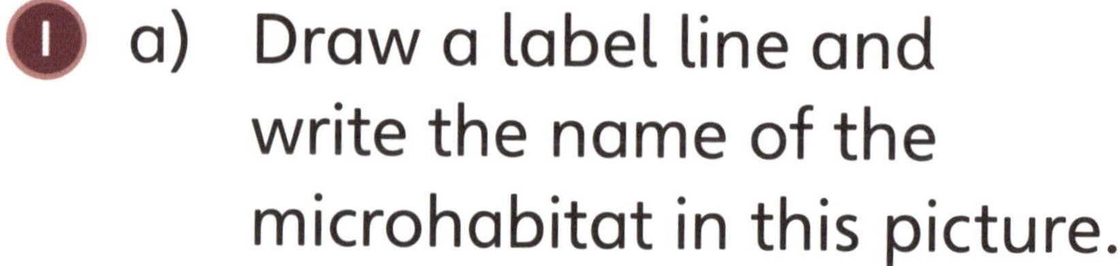

1. a) Draw a label line and write the name of the microhabitat in this picture.

b) Predict what this desert animal will do to stay cool.

____

2. This plant is growing on a road.

a) How is the road different in the place where the plant is growing?

____

b) What can the plant roots get in this microhabitat? _______________

c) Do you think plants can grow on the rest of the road? Give a reason.

____

3 This bird is looking into a hole in a tree.

   a) Write some words to describe what you think it is like inside the hole.

____

   b) Suggest why it is looking into the hole.

____

4 List any microhabitats you can see in this picture.

Start with words like **under** or **inside**.

____

____

____

____

____

Exploring habitats

1 Draw lines to match each animal with its habitat.

2 Write about a habitat you have explored outdoors.

Type of habitat

Date

Weather

Sunny or shady?

Draw some living things you saw.
Write their names and where
they were.

Animal adaptations

1 What does the word **adapted** mean?

____

2 a) What is a polar habitat like?

____

  b) List **three** adaptations that a polar bear has.

  1. ____

  2. ____

  3. ____

3 a) What is a desert habitat like?

____

  b) List **three** adaptations that a camel has.

  1. ____

  2. ____

  3. ____

4 The picture shows a howler monkey.

Draw lines to match each adaptation of the monkey with how it helps the monkey to survive.

brown colour	to curl around branches
long tail	to swing between trees
long arms	to find food
good sense of smell	to tell other monkeys about danger
makes a loud noise	to hide in trees

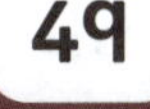

Plant adaptations

Class **2** draw some desert plants in pots.

1 a) Label the **spines** and the **pot** on this picture.

b) How do spines help this cactus to survive?

____

____

2 a) (i)   Where does this cactus store water?

____

(ii) Label this place on the picture.

b) Label the **flower** on this cactus.

Colour it a bright colour.

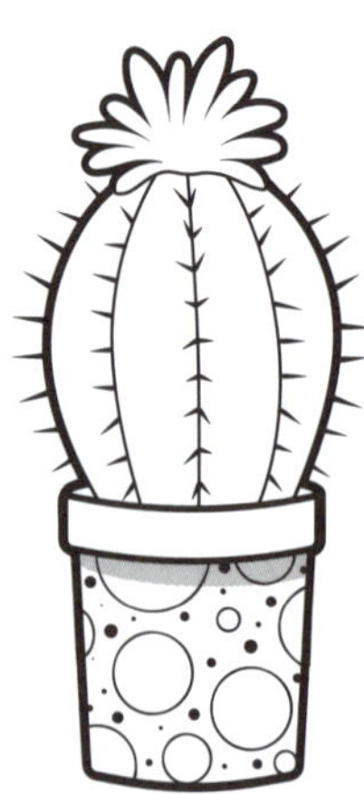

3 a) Label the **ridges** on this cactus.

b) How do ridges help this cactus to survive?

____

____

c) (i) Where are the **roots** of this cactus?

____

(ii) How do roots help a cactus to survive?

____

____

4 Label everything you can on this cactus.

1   a)   What do plants need to make their food?

1. _________________   2. _________________

3. _________________

b)   Which life process is making food?

____

c)   Which part of a plant traps sunlight?

____

2   a)   Label as many parts of this tree as you can.

b)   Draw a line across the picture to show which part of the tree is under the ground.

3 a) Name a plant that humans grow to get sugar.

____

b) In which part of this plant is the sugar found?

____

4 a) Humans get food from this potato plant. Label a **leaf**, the **stem** and a **potato**.

b) Draw a line across the picture to show which part is under the ground.

c) What food type do humans get from potatoes?

____

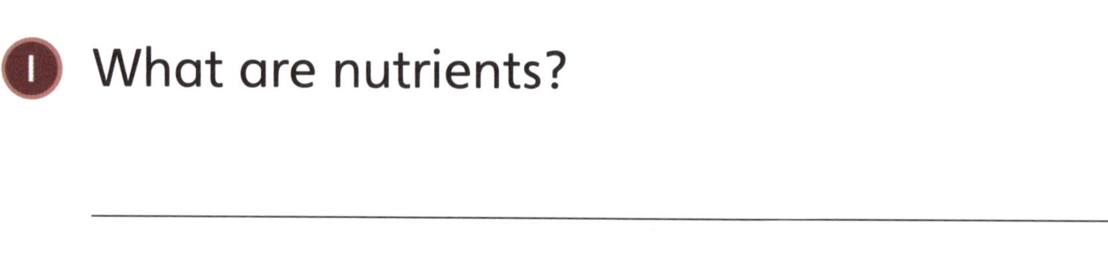

1 What are nutrients?

____

____

2 These living things live in grassland.

grass → gazelle → caracal → lion

a) What do scientists call places where animals and plants are found living?

____

b) What do the arrows on the diagram show?

____

c) What do gazelles eat? ___________________________

d) What does the diagram show the lion eats?

____

e) Lions also eat gazelles. Write a new food
    chain for **grass**, **gazelle** and **lion**.

3 The picture shows some living things.

a) How does maize make its food?

    ____

b) Mice eat maize. Owls eat mice.
    Write a food chain for **mice**, **maize** and **owl**.

c) The owl flies away, so the **snake** eats the
    mice instead.
    Write a new food chain for this.

Where can plants grow?

1   a)   What do plants need to stay alive?

1. ______________________   2. ______________________

3. ______________________

b)   What do scientists call things that affect where plants can grow?

e______________________   f______________________

2   Li has some plants.
One changes like this.

a)   Suggest why this has happened.

____

b)   What can Li do to stop this happening again?

____

c)   Another of Li's plants grows like this. Suggest why.

____

3 The picture shows two different plants, **A** and **B**.

a) Label the **roots** on each plant.

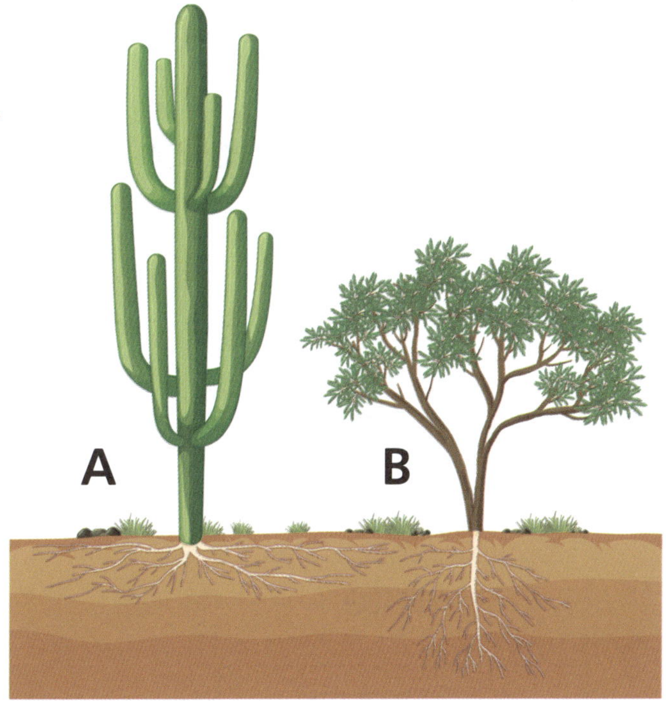

b) What do these plants use roots for?

____

c) Compare the roots of these two plants.

Use the words **longer** and **wider** in your answer.

____

____

____

1 Draw lines to match each animal with the place it can live.

whale

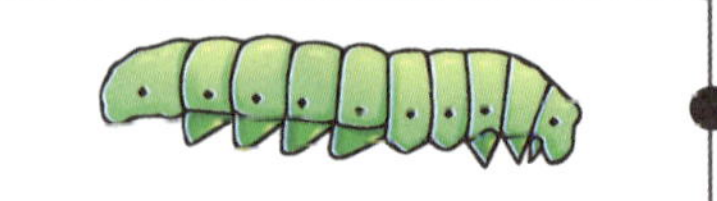

caterpillar

bird

frog

spider

2 A mole has big feet for **digging**.

a) Describe where the mole lives and what it is like inside.

____

____

____

____

b) Suggest how the mole makes this home.

____

____

What have I learned?

1. I understand the term **habitat** as the place where animals and plants are found living.

   I know this because I can name **two** different types of habitat.

   1. ________________________   2. ________________________

2. I understand that within a habitat there may be smaller **microhabitats**.

   I know this because I can name **two** different microhabitats.

   1. ________________________   2. ________________________

3. I can observe features of living things that suit them to a particular habitat.

   I can suggest how these adaptations help them to survive.

   I know this because I can write **two** features of a camel and how they help it to survive in a desert.

   1. ____

2. _______________________________________

4 I understand that living things may be interdependent.

I know this because I can write a food chain for a **rabbit**, a **fox** and some **grass**.

5 I understand that environmental factors may affect where animals and plants can live and how many live there.

I know this because I can name **three** environmental factors that plants need to grow well.

1. _______________________________________

2. _______________________________________

3. _______________________________________

I know that animals need to be able to find

f_________________ and w_________________ to

be able to survive.

Invertebrates

Invertebrates are animals without backbones. Invertebrates live in many different habitats. Worms and molluscs have soft bodies. Insects have a tough exoskeleton and three body parts.

In this topic we will learn:

- how to identify common invertebrates using pictures and simple keys
- to observe and describe the key features of common invertebrates
- to group invertebrates using features that they share
- to describe how some invertebrates change as they grow using simple life cycles.

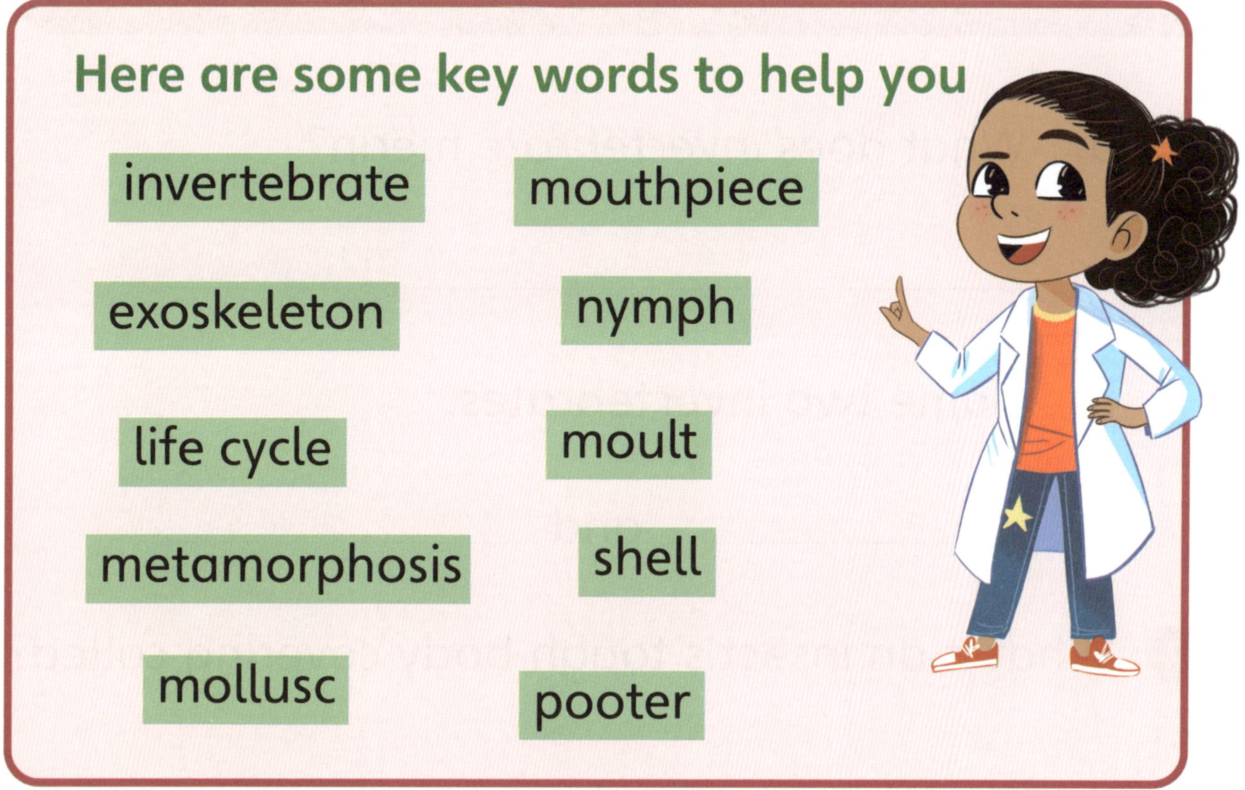

Choose two key words from the box above.
Write or draw what they mean.

Insects

1. a) What does *invertebrate* mean?

    ____

   b) Name **two** invertebrates.

    ___________________ and ___________________

2. What is an insect's tough body covering called?

    ____

3. a) Label each of these parts of the insect below.

   wing   **antenna**   **jointed leg**   **abdomen**

b)   Colour in **two** eyes.

c)   How many **antennae** does this insect have? ☐

d)   How many **wings** does this insect have? ☐

e)   How many **legs** do insects have? ☐

f)   To which body part are the wings and legs attached?

____

4   Label as many parts as you can on these two insect heads.

butterfly   bee

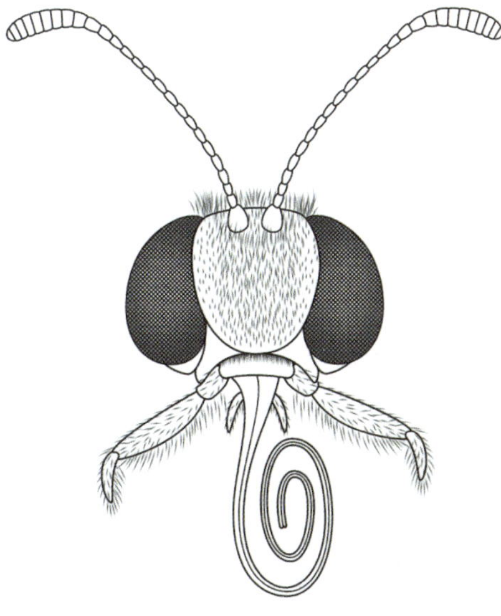

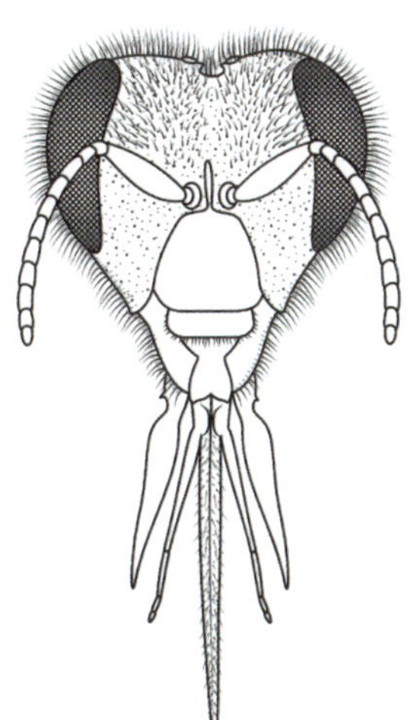

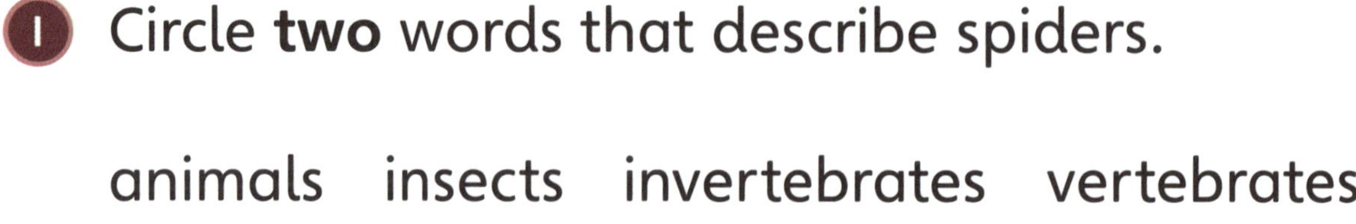

Spiders

1 Circle **two** words that describe spiders.

animals   insects   invertebrates   vertebrates

2 a) Name the **two** parts of a spider's body.

_______________________ and _______________________

b) (i) How many legs does a spider have?

c) (ii) To which body part are the legs attached?

____

c) Label these parts on the diagram.

jointed leg   abdomen   spinneret

3 a) What material do spiders use to make webs?

____

b) Why do some spiders make webs?

____

c) Design your own spider's web. Then draw a spider on it.

Look at the pictures above for help, but do not copy them.

1 a) Start at number 1 and join the numbered dots to draw a crab.

Curve each line a little to get the curved body shape you can see in your textbook.

b) Label these parts.

pincer   **hard exoskeleton**   **jointed leg**

2 Mia counts woodlice in four trays of leaves. Complete the tally chart for her results. 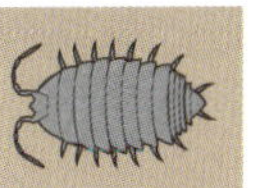

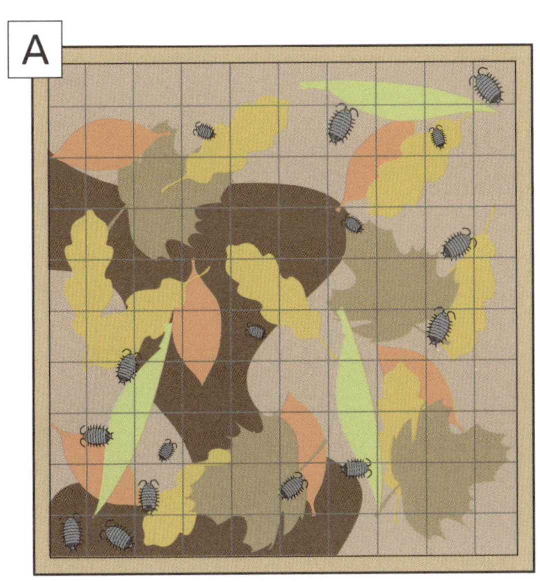

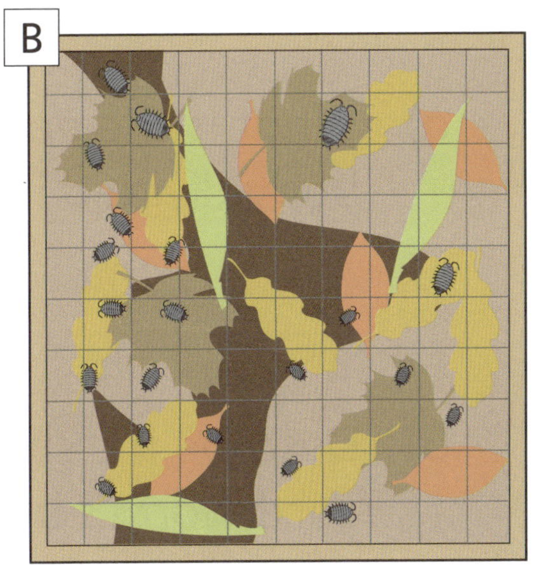

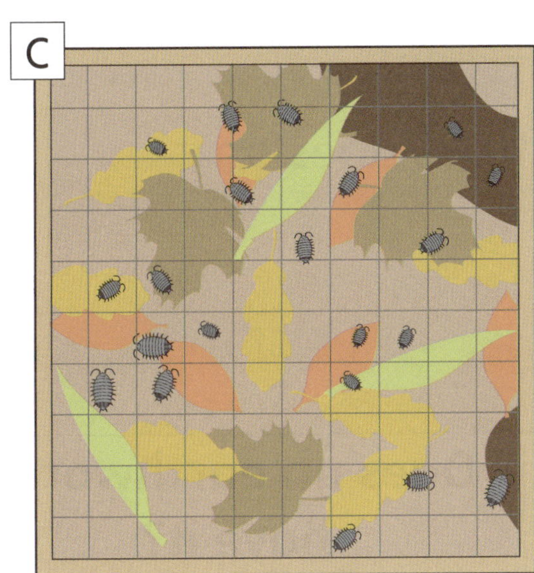

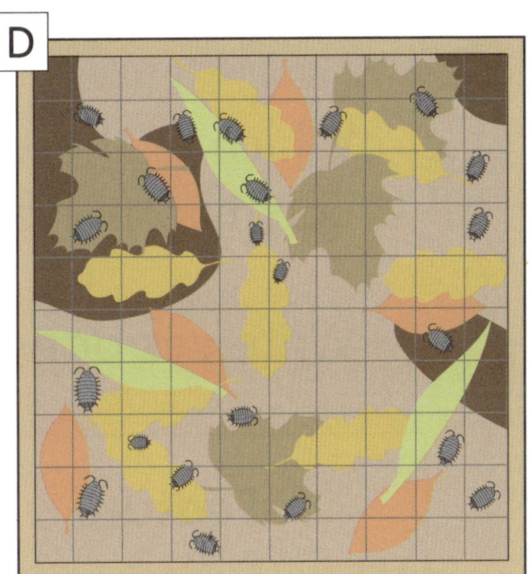

Tray	Number of woodlice	
	Tally	Totals
A		
B		
C		
D		

Worms

1. This is an earthworm.

    a)   What is the earthworm's body divided into?

       ____

    b)   Describe the shape of the earthworm's body.

       ____

    c)   Which of these features does an earthworm have?

       Write **yes** or **no**.

Feature	Does an earthworm have it?
legs	
wings	
eyes	
mouth	
hard body covering	

2 This is a leech. It is in the same animal group as an earthworm.

sucker to stick to the skin of other animals

a) Write **two** ways in which the leech and the earthworm are **similar**.

1. _________________________ 2. _________________________

b) Write **one** way in which they **differ**.

____

3 This snake is **not** in the same animal group as an earthworm.

a) Which animal group is a snake in?

____

b) Write **two** features that a snake has but an earthworm does **not**.

1. _________________________ 2. _________________________

Starfish

1 The picture shows some invertebrates and some invertebrate shells.

a) Circle all the **starfish**.

b) How many arms does every starfish in the picture have?

c) This is a starfish arm showing tube feet.

Which life process do starfish use tube feet to do?

____

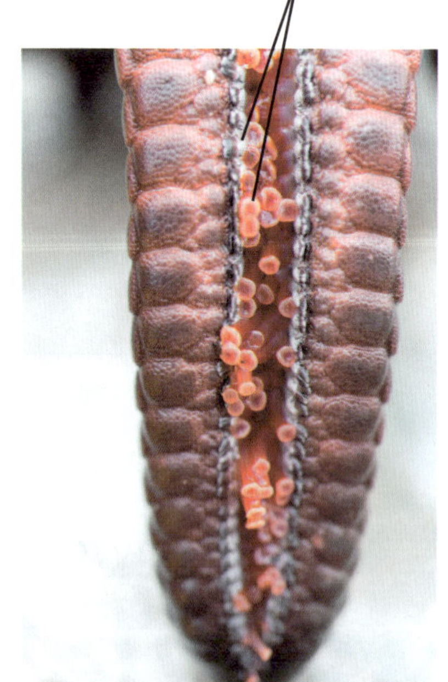

d) Circle the place where tube feet are found.

on top   underneath   on both sides

2 Starfish can grow new arms. We start with one starfish and finish with two.

Below, draw these starfish with all their arms grown back.

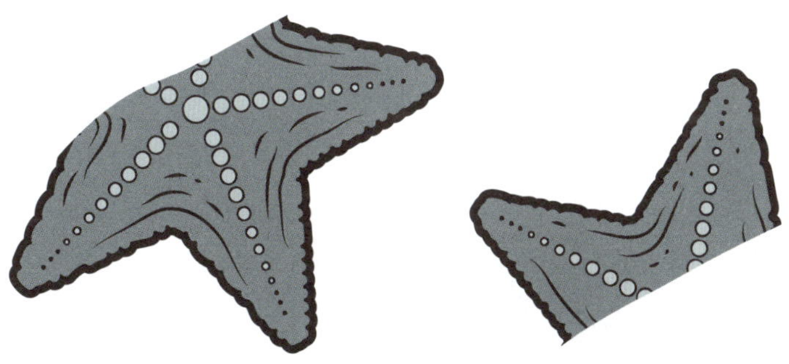

Molluscs

1 Which of these features do slugs and snails have?

Write **yes** or **no** in **every** box.

Feature	snail	slug
legs		
wings		
shell		
soft body		
antennae		

2 Deepesh finds some shells. Circle the **mussel**.

3 Elena draws this mollusc.

a) Complete the title to show which mollusc it is.

My drawing of _______________________

b) Label as many features as you can.

Draw a line and write the word each time.

c) What is this mollusc's habitat? _______________

d) Name **two** molluscs that look very similar to the one in the drawing.

_______________ **and** _______________

Invertebrate key

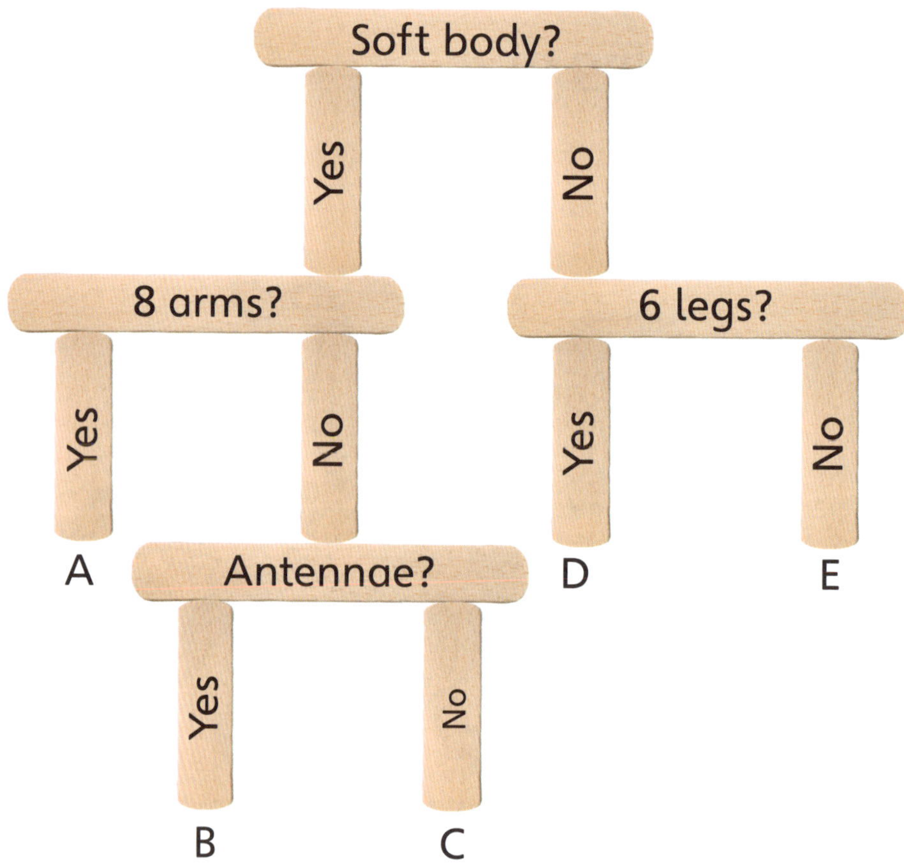

2 Use the key to write letter **P**, **Q**, **R**, **S** or **T** under each animal picture.

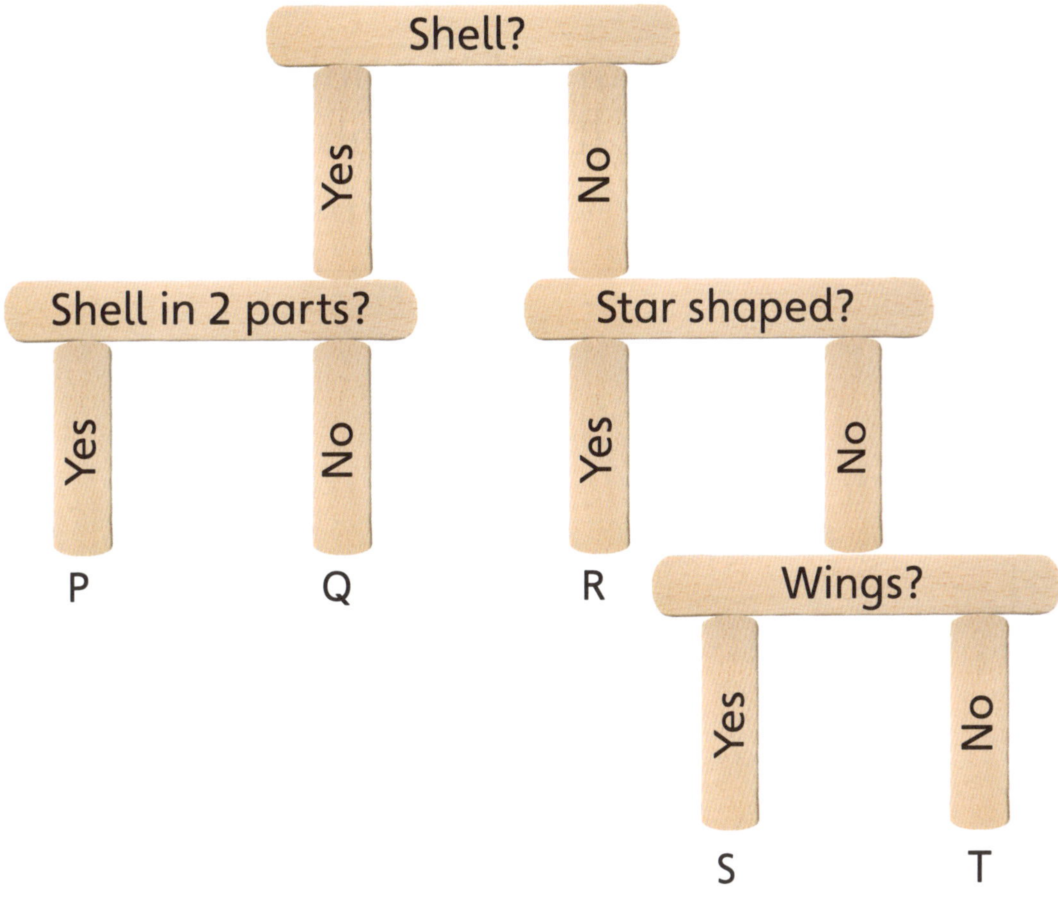

Looking for invertebrates

Explore a habitat near your home or school.

1. Choose a small part of the habitat and draw a picture of what it is like. Label the things you draw.

2. Circle all the words that describe the habitat when you were there.

all sunny   all shady   sunny and shady

cold   warm   hot   very hot

windy   rainy   muddy   dry

3 a) Are there animals living there that you did not see?

____

____

____

b) Which invertebrates did you see? Where did you see them? Draw and write about them.

____

____

____

Complete change

1 a)   Complete the title of this diagram.

The _____________ _____________ of a butterfly

b)   Write each word next to the correct picture.

pupa   adult   egg   caterpillar

c)   (i)   What does the caterpillar eat?

____

(ii)   What does the adult eat?

____

d)   What is this complete change called?

____

2 The pictures show how a mosquito changes as it grows.

a) Draw the missing arrows.

b) Write each word next to the correct picture.

eggs   pupa   adult   larva

c) Where does the adult mosquito lay her eggs?

____

d) How does the adult move?

____

e) Where do the larva and pupa live?

____

Incomplete change

1 a) Label the parts of this insect using lines and the words.

> antenna   thorax   wing   mouthparts
>
> head   eye   abdomen   jointed leg

b) Which part shows it is an **adult** insect?

____

2 a) Complete the sentence.

When insects change gradually as they grow it is called

_______________________________.

b) Where does an adult locust lay her eggs?

____

c) This is a locust nymph.

(i) What is the nymph's body covering called?

____

(ii) What must the nymph do to its body covering to become an adult?

____

d) What is another name for locust nymphs?

____

What have I learned?

1 I can identify a variety of common invertebrates using pictures and simple keys.

I know this because I can name these invertebrates.

2 I can observe and describe the key features of common invertebrates.

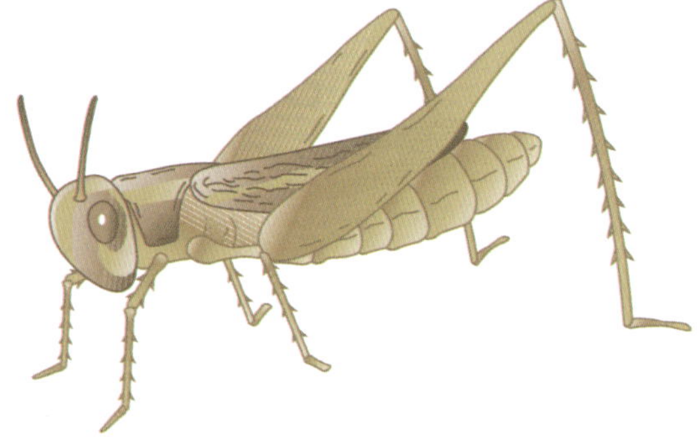

I know this because I can observe **six** features of this insect.

1. _______________   2. _______________

3. _______________   4. _______________

5. _______________   6. _______________

3 I can group invertebrates using features that they share.

I know this because I can write the animal group that each of these invertebrates are in.

4 I can describe how some invertebrates change as they grow using simple life cycles.

I know this because I can draw a life cycle for a butterfly and name the stages.

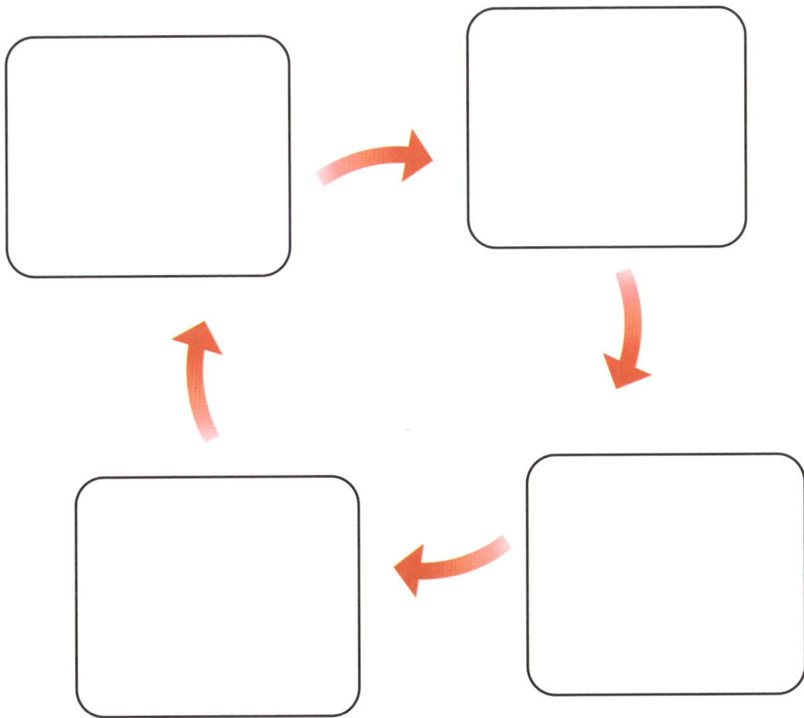

Materials: properties and uses

Humans use lots of different materials. Different materials have different uses. What we use a material for depends on its properties.

In this topic we will learn:

- that the same object can be made from lots of different materials
- that materials have different properties
- how to compare natural materials with human made materials
- how to use the properties of materials to group them
- how to do investigations that compare the properties of materials
- how to do investigations that are fair tests.

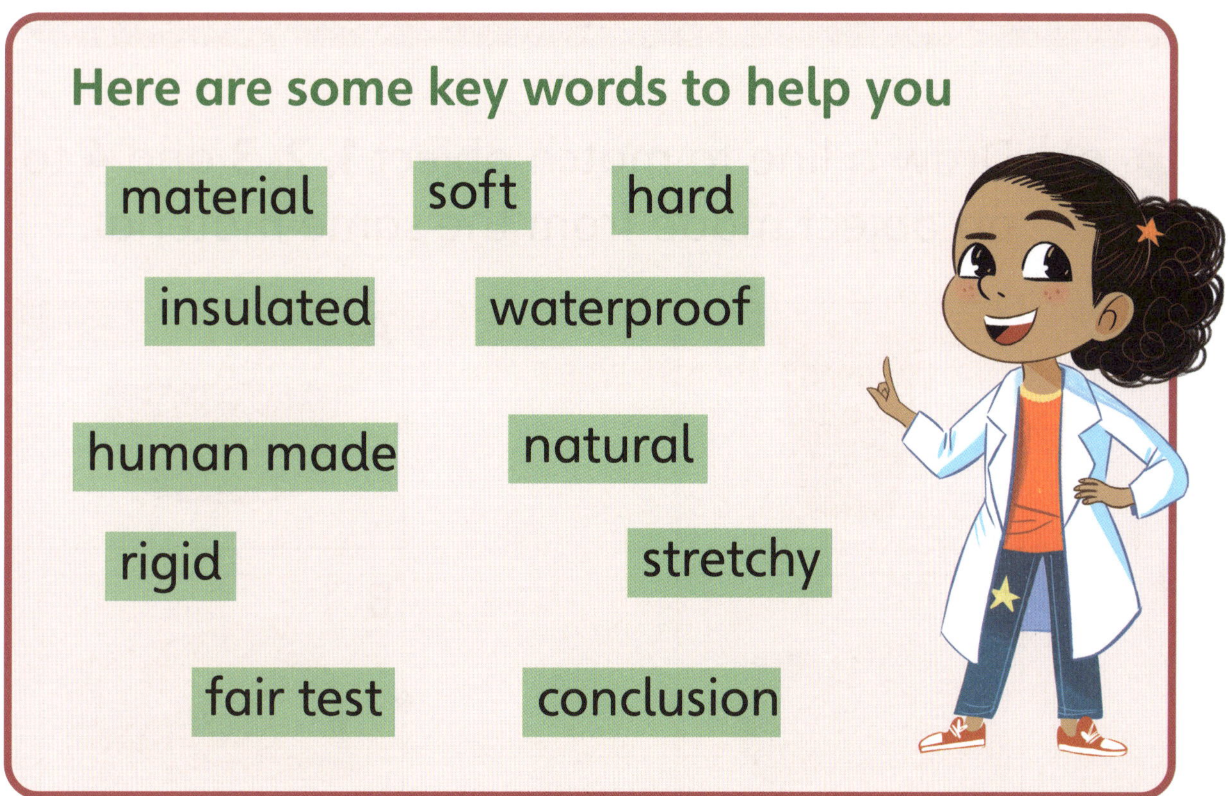

Choose two key words from the box above.
Write or draw what they mean.

Different materials

1 a) Draw a line to match object **1**, **2**, **3** and **4** to an object made from the same material.

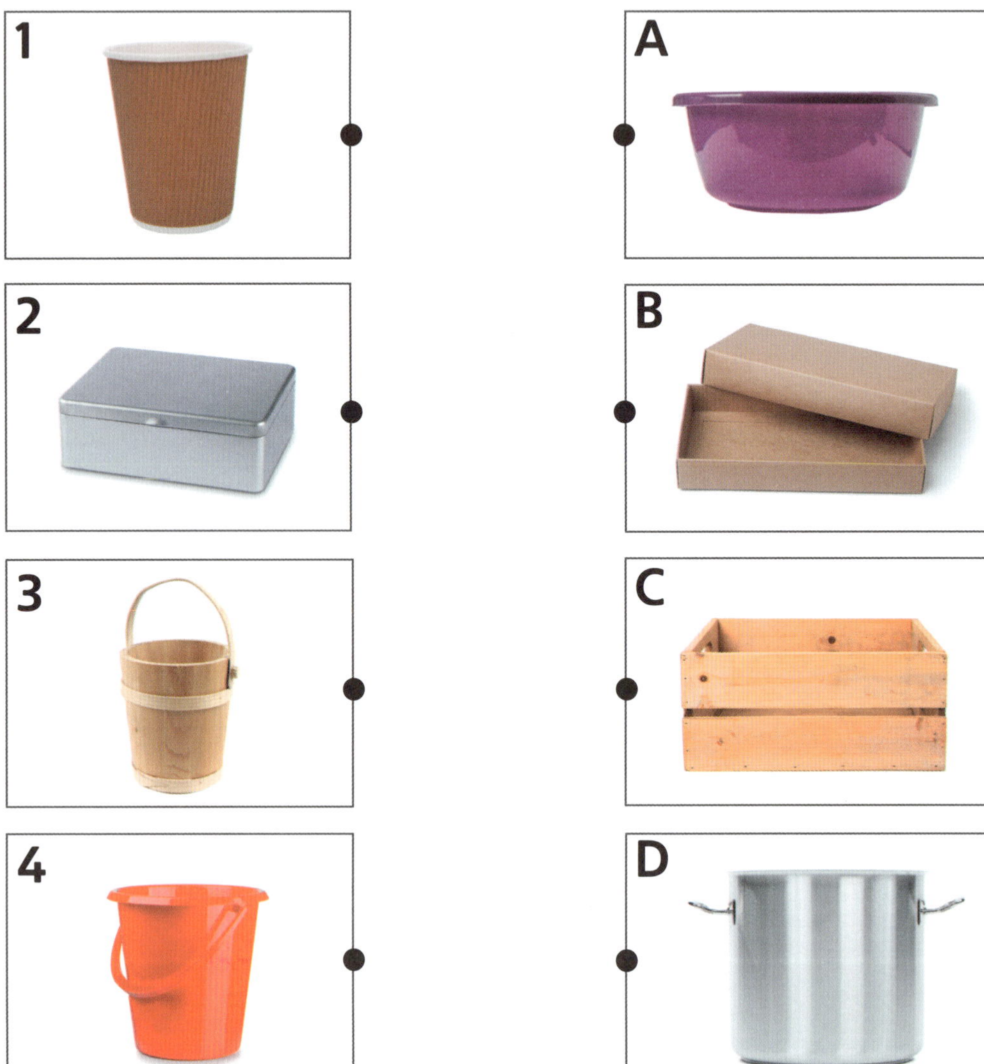

b) Write **one** number in each box to answer the questions about objects **1**, **2**, **3** and **4**.

(i) Which object is made of plastic? ☐

(ii) Which object is made of wood? ☐

c)   Look at objects **A**, **B**, **C** and **D**.

What material is each object made of?

A ________________   B ________________

C ________________   D ________________

2 Label the materials used to make these chairs.

Natural materials

1 Draw a line from each object to show whether it is made of a natural material or not.

made of a
natural
material

not made of
a natural
material

2 a) Tick (✓) all the **natural** materials.

cotton		stone	
nylon		plastic	

b) What animal makes natural silk?

____

c) Name **two** animals that give us wool.

1. _______________________   2. _______________________

d) (i) Where do we get cotton from?

____

(ii) Draw some clothes made from cotton.

Properties of wool

1 a) Which part of a sheep is its wool?

____

b) Why do sheep have wool?

____

____

c) How do we get the wool off the sheep?

____

d) Write **two** things about wool that help sheep live in cold and wet places.

1. ________________________ 2. ________________________

e) Circle **two** words that best describe wool.

hard   soft   stiff   shiny   stretchy

2 a) What do we do to find the answer to a scientific question?

____

b) Tick (✓) all the **scientific** questions.

What colour is a sheep?	
How much does wool cost in a shop?	
Does wool keep things warmer than cotton?	
Can wool dry faster than other materials?	
Do I like woolly clothes?	

3 Draw some clothes made from wool.

Testing properties: keeping warm

1 Class 2 test some materials to see if they keep things warm. The teacher cooks three potatoes.

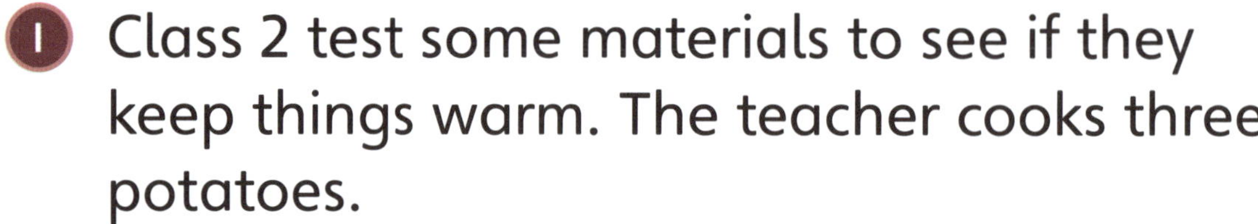

A 		B 		C 	
shiny foil		kitchen paper		no material	

She measures how hot each potato is at the start, then wraps two of them in different materials.

a) Complete the sentences. The teacher cooks potatoes that are the same

_______________.

This is to make the investigation a

_______________ _______________.

The scientific question is:

Which _______________ keeps

_______________ the warmest?

b) Predict which potato will be the warmest after 10 minutes. _______________________

c) Circle the equipment that measures how warm the potatoes are.

beaker   scales   thermometer   scissors

2 a) Complete the results table.

Material	Temperature in °C		
	At start	After 10 minutes	Change
shiny foil	50	47	3
kitchen paper	51	41	
no material	49	35	

b) (i) Which material gave the smallest change in temperature?

____

(ii) Which material keeps potatoes the warmest?

____

Building a house

1 Write **two** things a house protects us from.

1. _________________________   2. _________________________

2 a) Why do houses have windows?

____

b) Name **one** material used for windows.

____

3 Draw a picture of your house. Label any materials you know.

4 a) Name **one** material used for a roof.

____

b) Why is this a good material?

____

5 The walls of a house can be made of bricks.

a) Draw **one** brick in the space below.

b) Why is brick a good material for a wall?

____

c) These bricks are in a wall. Draw some more
of the wall.

Inside a home

1 Draw a line from each object to show a good material to make it from.

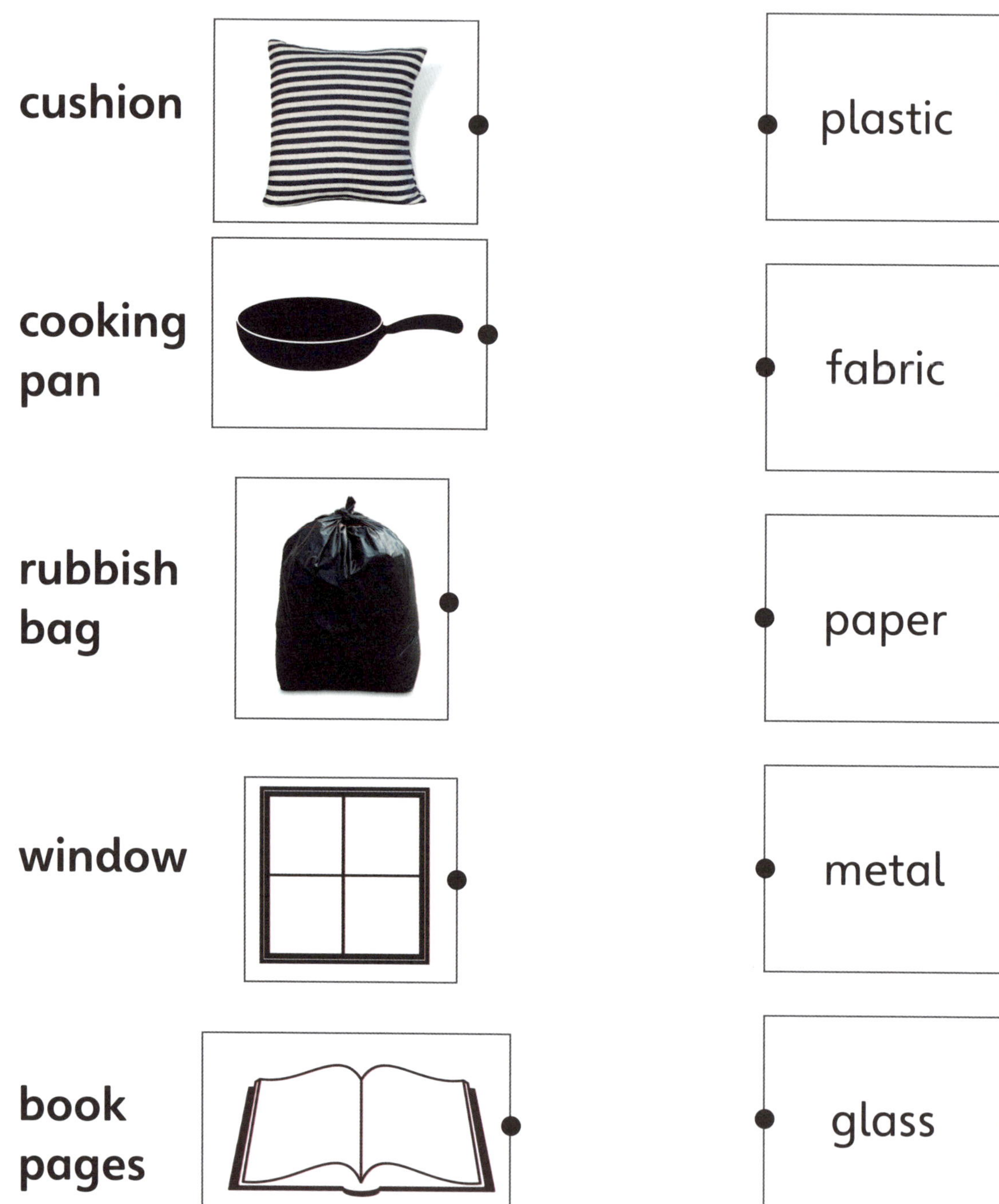

2 This bottle is made of chocolate.

a) Write **one** reason why chocolate is **not** a good material to use to make a bottle.

____

b) Name **two** materials that would be better than chocolate for making a bottle.

1. ___________________________   2. ___________________________

3 This T-shirt is made from fabric.

Draw T-shirts made from these other materials, to show what they would be like.

glass	**metal**	**bricks**

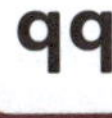

Testing properties: absorbing water

1. This sponge is absorbent.
What does *absorbent* mean?

____

2. Fatim tests three materials to see how much water they can absorb.

A	B	C
		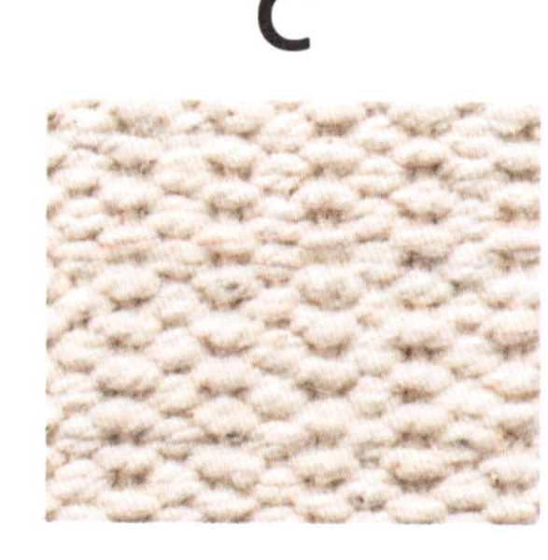

Complete the sentences in parts a) to c).

a) Fatim's scientific question is:

Which _________________ can _____________

the most _______________?

b) Fatim cuts pieces of _________________

that are the _______________ size. She

does this to make it a _________________

_______________.

c)   Fatim drops _________________ on each

material in turn. She _________________

how many drops of _________________ each

material can _________________.

d)   Write a heading for each column of the
results table.

A	20
B	2
C	10

e)   Which material absorbed the least water?

____

f)   Write a conclusion that answers Fatim's
scientific question.

____

____

____

Grouping materials

1. Find some objects made of different materials. Draw them in the circles.

hard objects

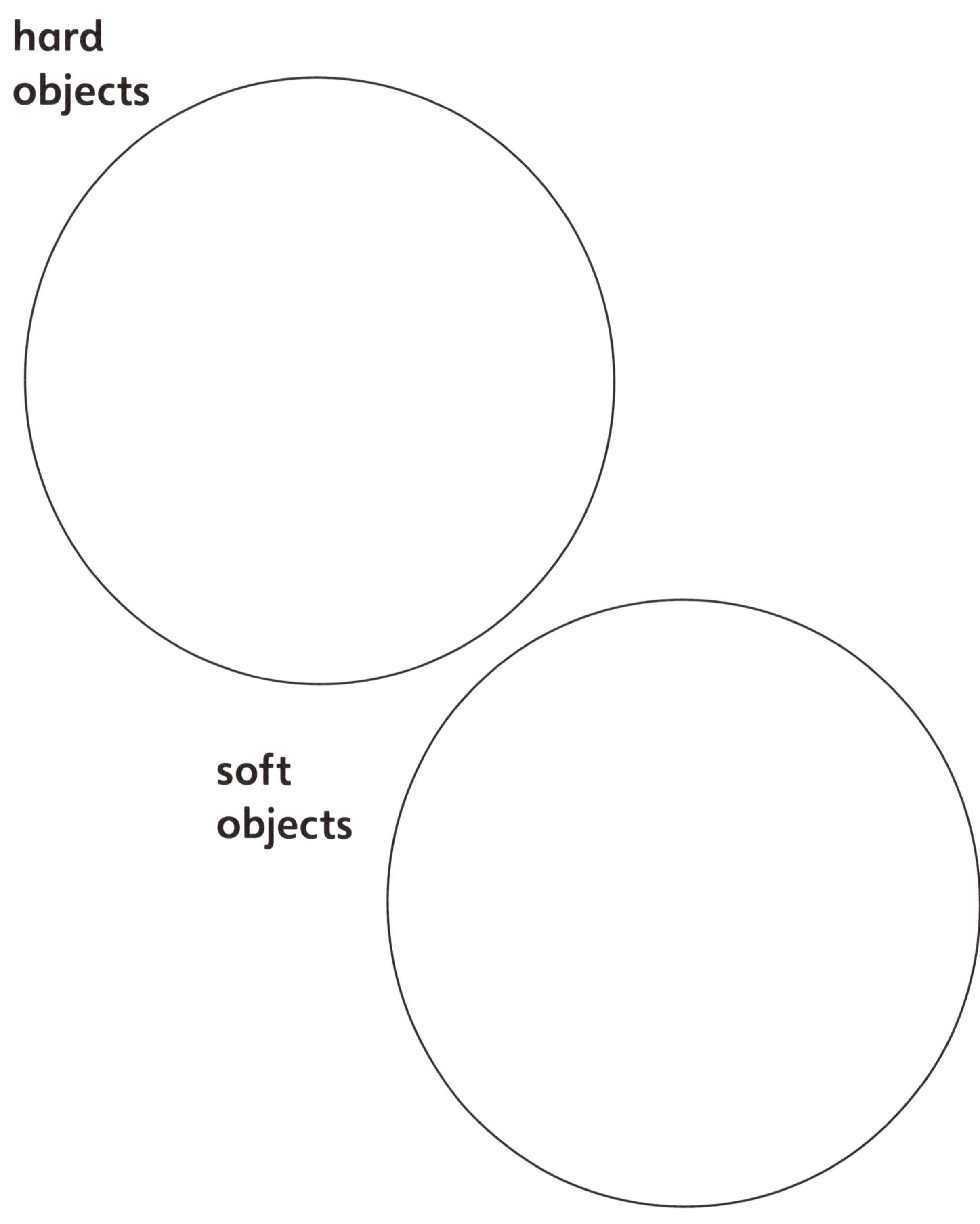

soft objects

2 Now find some objects to sort into these groups.

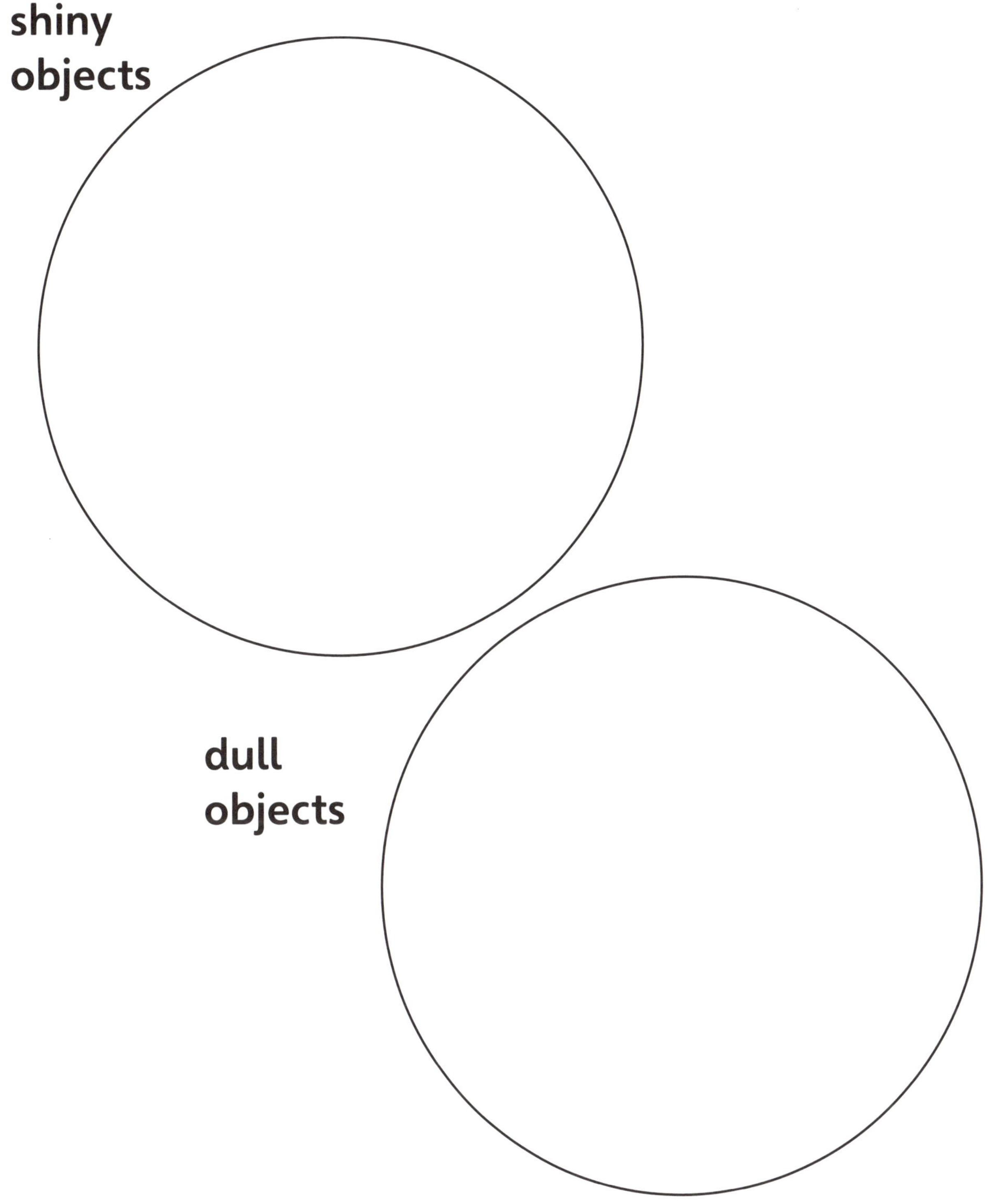

Choosing the right materials

1 Complete the drawing of this bear. Draw it wearing the clothes you thought of for the toy bear in the textbook.

  a) Draw the rest of its body yourself.

  b) Label the clothes to describe what they are made from.

2 a) Draw the bear dressed for a different activity.

b) Label the clothes to describe what they are made from.

What have I learned?

1. I understand that the same object can be made from lots of different materials.

   I know this because a bag can be made from:

   1. _________________   2. _________________

   3. _________________

2. I can compare natural materials with human made materials.

   I can name **two** different natural materials.

   1. _________________   2. _________________

3. I understand that some properties of materials make them more suited to a use.

   I know this because I can name a material to make each of these things from:

window	door	cooking pot	cushion

4 I can use the properties of materials to group them.

______________________ or soft

______________________ or dull

rough or ______________________

5 I can justify choosing a material for a use by thinking of its properties.

I can complete these sentences.

Fabric is used for clothes because it is

______________________.

Metal is used for rings because it is

______________________.

6 I can do investigations that compare the properties of materials.

I can do investigations that are fair tests. For a fair test I must only change ______________________ thing and keep everything else the ______________________.

Sound

Something that makes a sound is a sound source. There are many different sources of sound. Engines often make loud sounds that get quieter as we move away from them. Musical instruments make sounds when we hit, pluck or shake them.

In this topic we will learn:

- that a source is the place where a sound starts from
- how to identify and describe sounds that are made in different ways
- that loud sounds may damage our hearing
- that sounds travel from a source to our ears
- how sounds can be made louder or quieter.

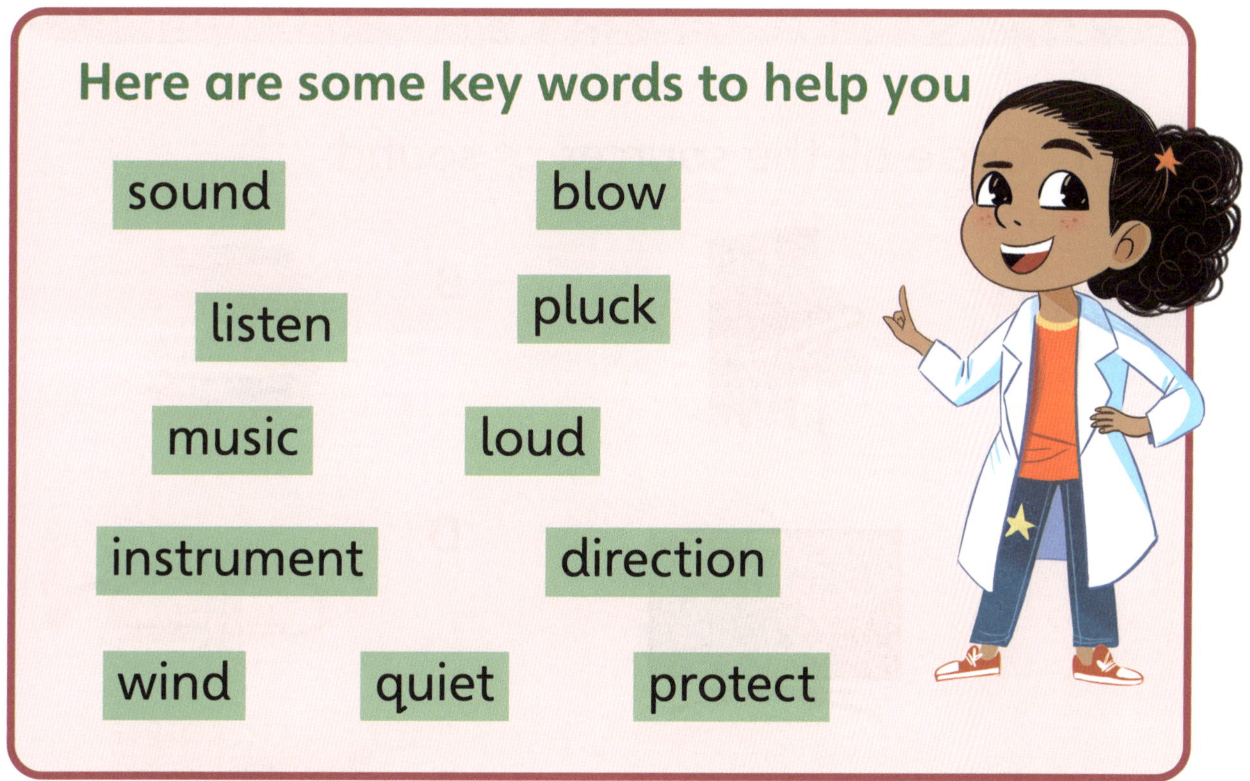

Choose two key words from the box above.
Write or draw what they mean.

Sound sources

1 a) Circle all the sources of sound.

A

B

C

D

E

F

G

H

b) Which letter shows a **living thing** that is a source of sound?

____

c) Which **two** letters show objects with **engines** that make the sound?

__________   __________

2 Draw some sources of sound from your **classroom**, **outside** or **home**.

Name each sound source you draw and the place it is in.

Wind instruments

1. a) Name **two** wind instruments.

    _______________ and _______________

    b) Circle **one** word that shows how to play a wind instrument.

    hit   blow   rub   bend

    c) What moves through a wind instrument to make a sound?

    ____

    d) Name **two** materials used to make wind instruments.

    _______________ and _______________

    e) Name this instrument.

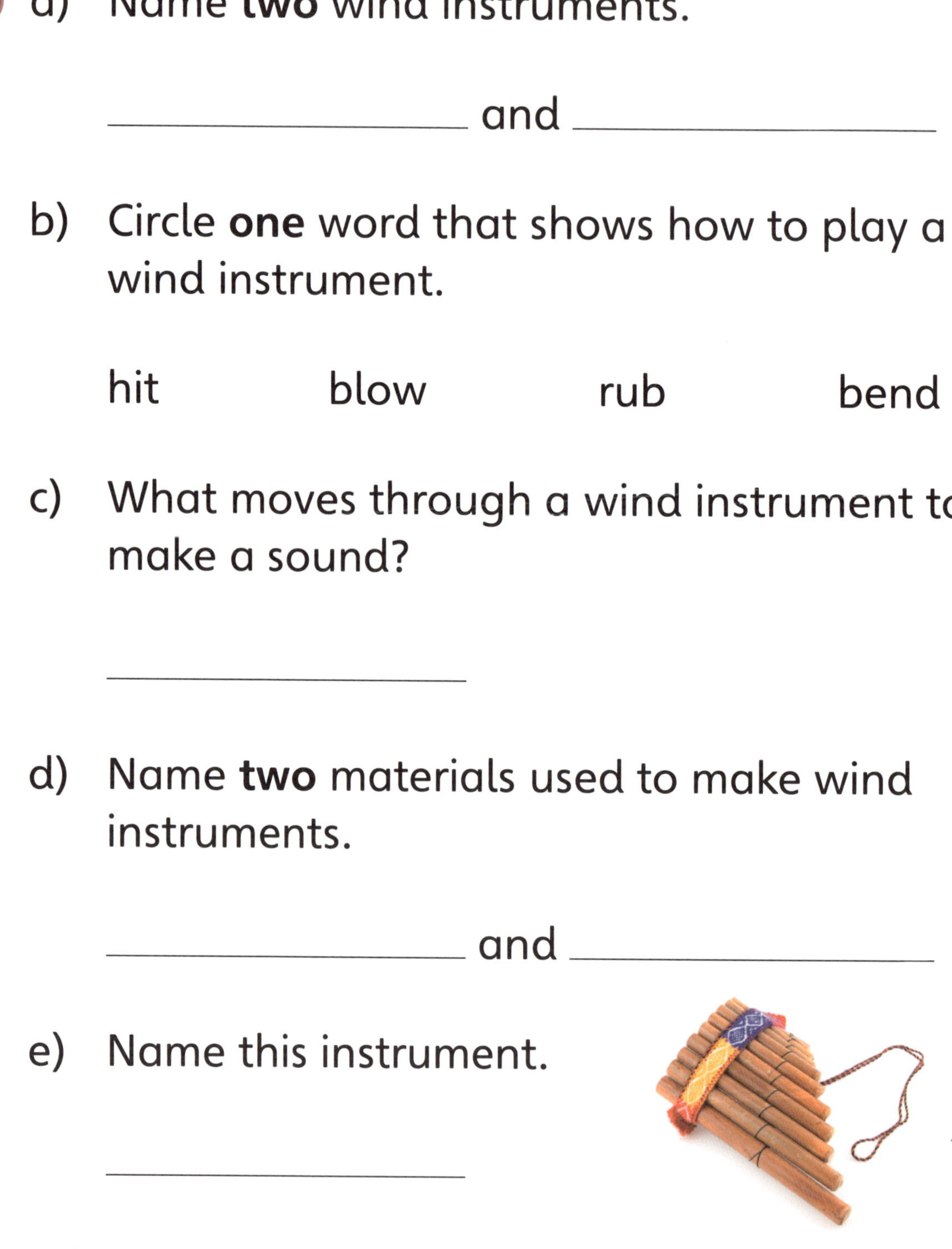

    ____

2. Which sense organ do we use to listen to music?

    ____

3 a) Draw you or a friend or someone in your family playing a musical instrument.

or

Draw somewhere you go where musical instruments are played.

b) Write one or two sentences to describe what is happening in your picture.

Percussion instruments

1 Percussion instruments are sources of sound when they are hit or shaken.

Write **hit**, **shake** or **both** under each instrument.

2 Make a percussion instrument like the drum in your textbook.

a) Draw your instrument.

b) Label the parts to show how you made it.

c) Can you change the sound it makes? Describe how.

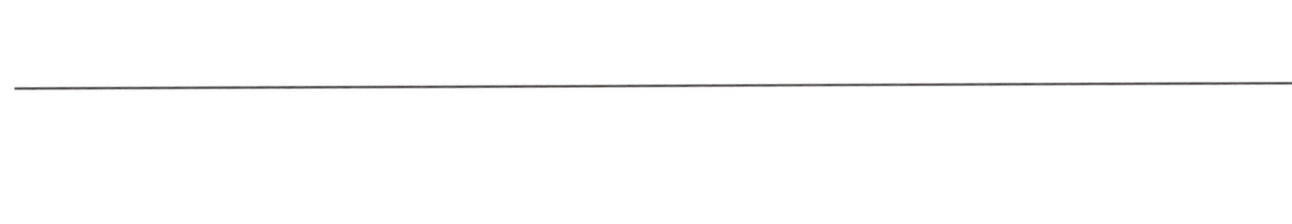

Making more sounds

1 a) Circle **one** instrument that is plucked to make a sound.

b) What does *plucked* mean?

____

____

c) What do instruments that are plucked all have?

____

2 Describe **two** ways to make a sound with this violin.

1. ____

2. ____

3 Make an instrument using elastic bands.

There are some ideas in your textbook.

a) Draw your instrument.

b) What can you do to the elastic bands to make the sound change?

Find as many ways as you can.

Hearing sounds

1 a) Circle **two** sources of sound.

radio	book	drill	pencil	jug

b) Which sense organ is used for hearing?

____

c) How does sound reach our sense organ from the source?

____

2 Cai and Ada make a string telephone.

It does **not** work very well.

Describe **two** ways they could improve their string telephone.

____

____

3 Write **one** letter for each answer.
Use each letter once.

a) Who is trying to hear sounds better? _______

b) Who cannot hear sounds? _______

c) Who is telling people to stop making sounds? _______

d) Who is trying to stop making a sound?

____

e) Who is a source of sound? _______

Loud and quiet sounds

1 a) Colour things that make loud sounds **red**.

b) Write a word to describe the sound the other things make.

____

2 Ceri sees this at work.

a) What sort of sounds will she hear?

____

b) How could the sounds at work be harmful to Ceri?

____

c) Circle **two** pieces of equipment that help Ceri stay safe from noise at work.

Where is the sound?

1 **a)** Circle the sense organ that we use to listen to sounds.

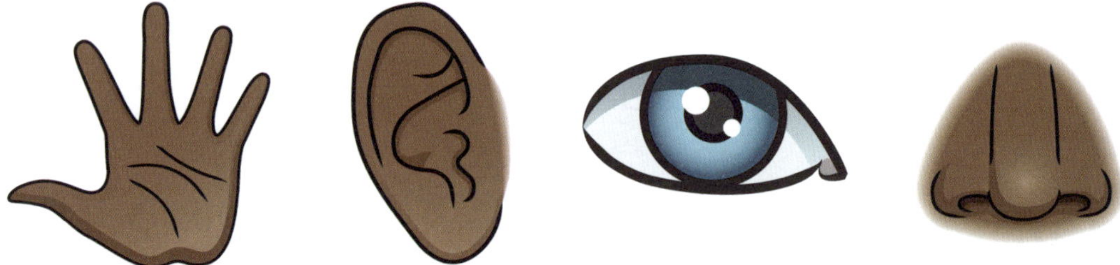

b) Which sense do we use to listen to sounds?

____

c) Circle **two** reasons that we have **two** ears.

to listen to sounds getting louder	to hear sounds on both sides of our head
to make quieter sounds	to compare with a partner the sounds we can hear
to compare sounds going to each ear	

d) We can see part of our ear on the side of our head. Where is the rest of the ear?

____

2 a) Make this head look like the top of yours.

b) Listen to sounds in your classroom or outside.

Write the sounds that you hear all around the picture of your head.

Put the words in the position each sound is coming from.

How far away is the sound?

1 a) Circle all the **sources** of sound.

b) Complete the sentences.

Sounds travel through the ________________
from a ________________ of sound.

When the sound reaches our ________________
we can ________________ the sound.

2 Nia plays some music. Her friends listen.

Nia  

a) Write **L** under the friend who hears her the **loudest**.

b) Write **Q** under the friend who hears her the **quietest**.

c) Ava stands at different distances from Nia.

(i) Why must Nia stay in the same place?

____

(ii) Complete the sentences.

At 10 steps away the sound Ava hears is

______________ than at [ ] steps away.

At 40 steps away the sound is

______________ than at [ ] steps away.

What have I learned?

1 I understand the word *source* means the place where a sound starts from.

I know this because I can name **three** different sound sources.

1. ___________________   2. ___________________

3. ___________________

2 I can identify and describe sounds that are made in different ways from different types of source.

I can name **three** different sound sources that are things with **engines**.

1. ___________________   2. ___________________

3. ___________________

I can name **two percussion** instruments.

1. ___________________   2. ___________________

I can name **two wind** instruments.

1. ___________________   2. ___________________

3 I understand that loud sounds may damage hearing.

I know this because I can draw what people who work in noisy places should wear.

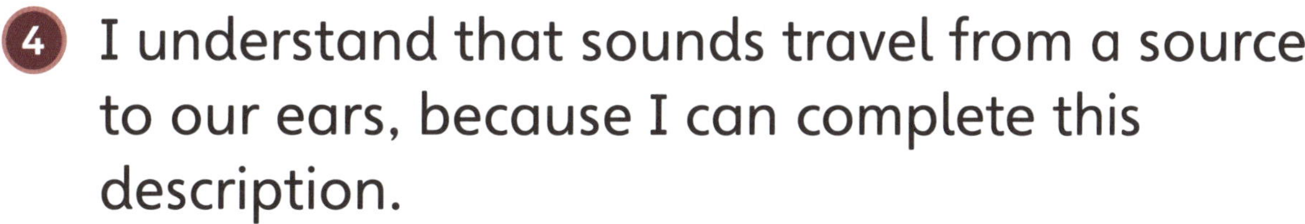

4 I understand that sounds travel from a source to our ears, because I can complete this description.

Sounds travel through the __________________

from a __________________ of sound to our ears.

We have two ears so we can hear sounds

coming from __________________ directions.

5 I can explain how sounds can be made louder or quieter by changing the distance from the source.

If I walk away from a sound source, the sound

gets __________________.

If I walk towards a sound source, the sound

gets __________________.

Space

The Earth, Sun and Moon are part of our Solar System. Our Sun is just one of many stars in space. We can see other distant stars in the night sky.

In this topic we will learn:

- that the Earth, Sun and Moon are part of our Solar System
- how the shape of the Moon appears to change over time
- that the Sun is one of many stars in space and that stars can form constellations
- about astronauts and space travel.

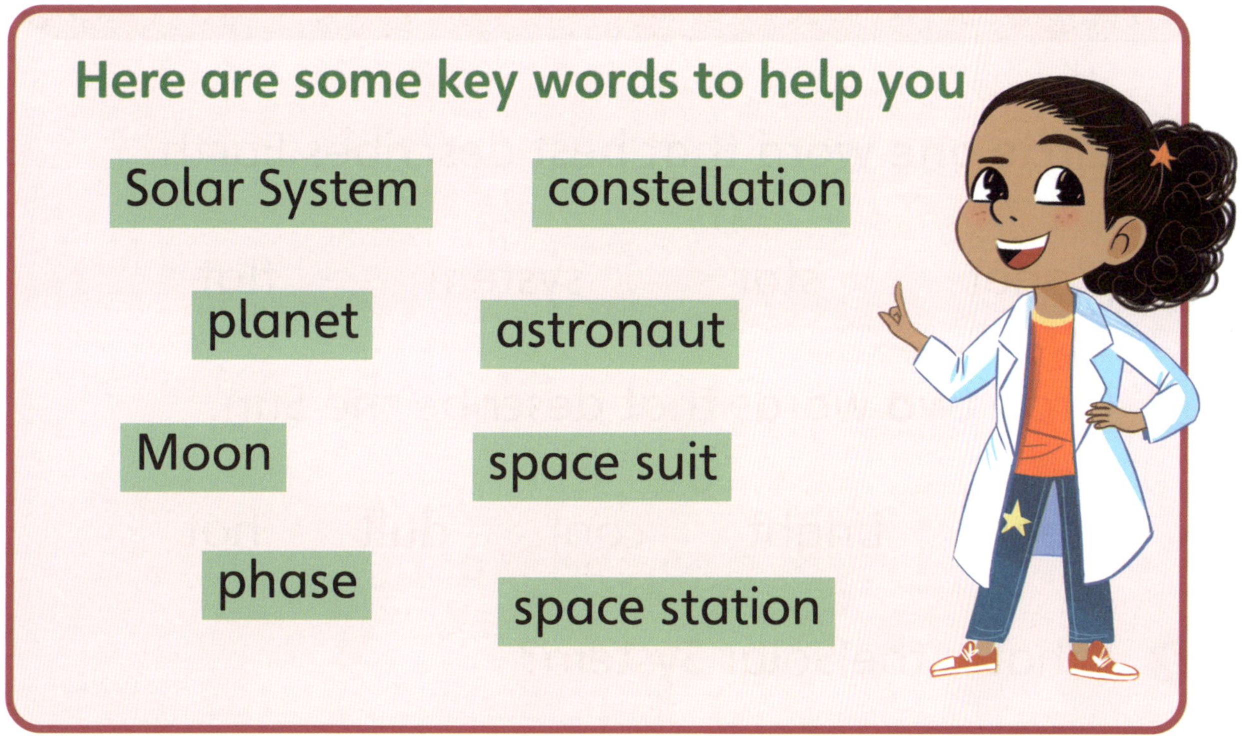

Choose two key words from the box above.
Write or draw what they mean.

Our Solar System

1. Circle **one** word that best describes Earth.

   planet   star   system   flat

2. Circle **two** words that describe the Sun.

   green   bright   cool   dull   hot

3. What is the Solar System?

   ____

   ____

4. Look at the picture of Earth on the next page.

   a) Can you find a country?

       Draw a label line and write its name.

   b) Draw a label line and write the word to
       label each of these things.

       ocean   **land**   **cloud**

131

Our moon

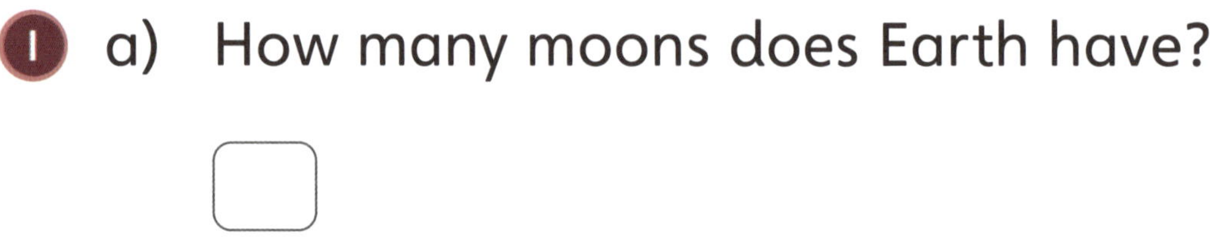

1 a) How many moons does Earth have?

b) Which is bigger, Earth or the Moon?

____

c) What are Earth, the Sun and the Moon part of? Circle your answer.

Great Galaxy   Solar System

Planets Group   Space Station

2 Tick (✓) **two** correct statements.

The Sun moves round Earth.	
Earth moves round the Moon.	
The Moon moves round Earth.	
Earth spins as it moves round the Sun.	
The Sun moves round the Moon.	

3 The picture shows three objects in space, labelled **A**, **B** and **C**.

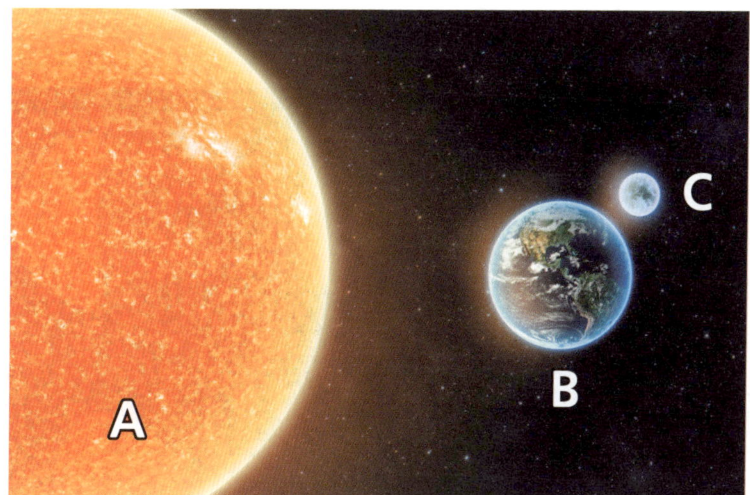

Name objects **A**, **B** and **C**.

A ___________________________   B ___________________________

C ___________________________

4 Look at the picture of the surface of the Moon in your textbook.
Describe what it is like.

____

____

____

Changing Moon

1. The diagrams show how the Moon looks to us on different days.

a) Each picture shows a different _____________ of the moon.

b) Picture 1 shows a new moon.

Which other picture shows a new moon?

c)   Draw a full moon.

d)   Which number matches this picture? 

2) Watch the Moon and colour in your moon diary to show what it looks like each day. Describe what you saw.

1. Choose words from the box to complete the sentences.

Each word may be used only once.

bright	ears	cold	burning	star
planet	moon	Solar	Sun	hot
eyes	largest	smallest	ball	dull

The Sun is a __________. It is the __________ object in our __________ System.

The Sun is very __________ and very __________. We never look at the Sun because it can damage our __________.

The Sun is made of a hot, glowing __________ of __________ gases.

2. Why does the Sun look bigger than the stars we see at night?

____

3 a) Draw a picture of what the Sun looks like. Use your textbook to help.

b) Draw a picture of a night sky with stars and the Moon.
Which phase of the Moon will you draw?

Constellations

1 The children are looking into the sky.

   a) Is it day or night? Give a reason.

      day ☐   night ☐

____

   b) Describe as fully as you can what the children are looking at.

____

____

____

   c) **(i)** What are they using to find out about the night sky?

____

      (ii) Write **one other** way they could find out about the night sky.

____

2 **a)** Describe the best sort of places to look at stars.

____

____

b) Find out what a telescope is used for and write about it here.

____

____

c) Look at the night sky from a window. Draw what you can see.

1 What does the word *astronaut* mean?

____

2 a) Why does it take a long time to become an astronaut?

____

____

b) Write about **two** different jobs that astronauts need to do in space.

1. _______________________________________

____

2. _______________________________________

____

c) (i) What are an astronaut's clothes called?

____

(ii) What is in the tank on the astronaut's back? _______________

(iii) Label the astronaut to show all the things they are wearing.

Draw a line and write words for each label.

Living and working in space

1. Which of these could take a person to a space station? Circle one.

2. This person is working in space. She is joined to a space station.

panels on the space station

a) What do we call a human who travels from Earth into space?

____

b) Why is this person joined to the space station?

____

c) What are the big panels on the space station used for?

____

____

d) Draw lines to match each object with the reason it is needed by a person in space.

helmet	protect hands
air tank	keeps body warm
water	to walk on rough surfaces
gloves	protects head and eyes
boots	to drink
space suit	to breathe

What have I learned?

1. I know that Earth, the Sun and the Moon are part of our Solar System.

I know this because I can label Earth, the Moon and the Sun in this picture.

I know that our Solar System is made of a

_______________ and the things like

_______________ that are near it.

2. I can describe how the shape of the Moon appears to change over time.

I can draw the **two** missing pictures here:

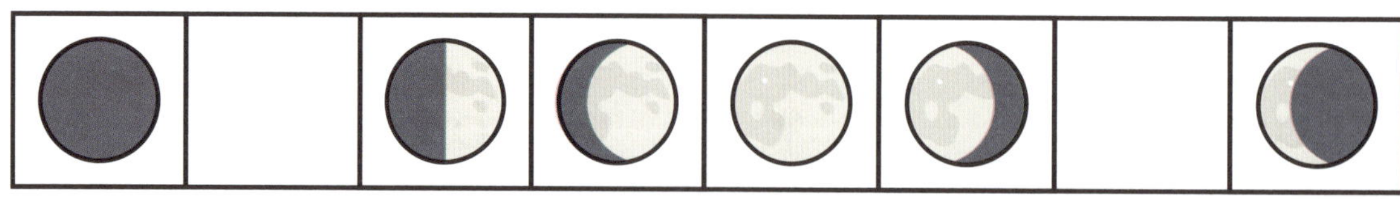

3 I know that the Sun is one of many stars in space and that stars can form constellations.

I know this because I can draw the pattern of **one** constellation.	

4 I understand the term *astronaut* and can describe space travel and what living in space is like.

a) An astronaut is a human who…

____

b) I can describe some things that an astronaut does in space.

____

____

____

____

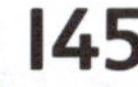

My notes

My notes

My notes

(key: b-bottom; c-centre; l-left; r-right; t-top)

Non-Prominent Image Credit(s):

123RF GB LIMITED: Suryadi Djasman Kartodiwiryo 58 L T-B 1, Anton Samsonov 118 L-R 3t, Frameangel 31 L-R 1b, Valentyna Chukhlyebova 46 L T-B 4, gayane1966 84 L-R 3t, schan 76 L-R 5b, Ivonne Wierink 112b, Maryana Lyubenko 84 L-R 4t, Volha Shaukavets 14c, 14c, 14c, 14c, 14c, Kittasgraphics 75, Avelkrieg 122t, Cathy Yeulet 18t, jessmine 89c; **GETTY IMAGES INCORPORATED:** MarcoGovel/iStock 26 L-R 3t, GOLFX/iStock 26 L-R 1t; **PEARSON EDUCATION:** Amit John 56b, Arvind Singh Negi/Red Reef Design Studio 58 L T-B 2, 58 R T-B 1, 85t, 58 L T-B 3, 80t, HL Studios 84c, 85t, 85t, Joey Chan 32t, PDQ Digital Media Solutions Ltd 56c, 135, 141, 85b, 58 L T-B 4, 58 L T-B 5, Sanjay Charadva 14c, Utsav Academy and Art Studio 85t; **SHUTTERSTOCK:** Irina Markova 46 R T-B 5, Panda Vector 33c, 33c, 33c, Sylverarts Vectors 32b, bonchan 8 L-R 1t, Mikhaylovskiy 13t, Daniel Heighton 121 4b, FoxyImage 125 L-R 1c, Photos SS 142 L-R 2t, NP27 98 T-B 3, Madiz 88 L T-B 2, GraphicsRF 110 L T-B 1, 110 R T-B 2, Anton Starikov 110 L T-B 3, Antonov Roman 46 L T-B 1, Oceloti 41t, Victor Moussa 121 2b, mything 14c, 14c, 14c, StockSmartStart 31 L-R 2b, BlueRingMedia 57t, 71t, 81t, Vaclav Volrab 74 L-R 1t, SeventyFour 29c, nahariyani 114 L-R 2b, Chros 24 L-R 4t, Ekaterina Kolomeets 124 3 L-R 2b, AKIllustration 122t, 122t, 122t, Maksym Bondarchuk 114 L-R 3t, Boonchuay1970 12 L-R 5t, Toey Toey 26 L-R 5t, falisdeka 120 L T-B 2, Nosyrevy 72t, Zhengzaishuru 76 L-R 3b, 84 L-R 2t, Pedjalaya 116 L-R 3t, aurelie le moigne 49t, ducu59us 18 T-B 4b, vtaurus 66b, 3drenderings 116b, abramsdesign 114 L-R 2t, bigacis 12 L-R 2t, Andrei Kuzmik 10 L-R 3t, Cosmin Manci 76 L-R 2b, Luka Hercigonja 45t, Ton Weerayut Photographer 90 T-B 4, Anton Starikov 16 T-B 4, magicinfoto 100 L-R 2c, Burdun Iliya 114 L-R 2c, Meggi 29t, Technicsorn Stocker 121t, Rattiya Thongdumhyu 72b, sbego 27t, FabrikaSimf 90 T-B 1, BNP Design Studio 125 L-R 2c, Koosen 8 L-R 4c, 88 R T-B 2, Eric Isselee 76 L-R 1b, Baishev 114 L-R 3c, Baanrukbua 20 L T-B 4, DenisMArt 8 L-R 1c, Pushba 88 L T-B 1, Slava_Kovtun 8 L-R 2c, THP Creative 98 T-B 2, Nmonicas 9 L-R 2b, stockphotofan1 99t, Gala_Kan 16 T-B 6, Ruslan Ivantsov 118 L-R 4t, frank_peters 124 2 L-R 3c, nednapa 26 L-R 4t, Vangert 24 L-R 1t, max dallocco 131, Givaga 77 L-R 2b, fizkes 22t, Oleon17 120 L T-B 3, photosync 121 1b, M.i.k.e 25c, Courtesy of Photo smile. 121 5b, Vitals 10 L-R 5t, EM Arts 10 L-R 1t, Birgit Reitz-Hofmann 124 3 L-R 3b, schankz 124 2 L-R 1c, inavanhateren 44t, Artush 46 R T-B 3, petrroudny43 15c, Cindy Shebley 114 L-R 1c, Holiday. Photo.Top 88 R T-B 1, riekephotos 46 R T-B 4, Arvind Balaraman 20 L T-B 3, Eric Isselee 74 L-R 2t, tanuha2001 110 R T-B 1, photokin 8 L-R 3c, Viktar Malyshchyts 16 T-B 2, Kavring 88 L T-B 3, DoublePHOTO studio 26 L-R 3t, fanta_c 29b, BearFotos 46 L T-B 3, Valentin Agapov 118 L-R 2t, Ann in the uk 41c, Antonina Sotnykova 114 L-R 1b, vlavetal 20 L T-B 2, Pixfiction 76 L-R 4b, Raura7 7t, 7t, 7t, 7t, 7t, 7t, 7t, 7t, 7t, 7t, 7t, 7t, 7t, 7t, wavebreakmedia 31t, Anton Starikov 88 L T-B 4, Mr. SUTTIPON YAKHAM 110 R T-B 4, Pixel-Shot 30t, 30t, 30t, 30t, 12 L-R 4t, Iurii Kachkovskyi 10 L-R 4t, D. Kucharski K. Kucharska 83c, John Orsbun 124 3 L-R 1b, Aphelleon 133, Ziablik 74b, SpeedKingz 19t, PROFFIPhoto 142 L-R 3t, Tetiana Mandziuk 22c, wk1003mike 90 T-B 3, No-Te Eksarunchai 26 L-R 2t, Hortimages 16 T-B 3, Kazakova Maryia 59t, Design tech art 7 L-R 2c, 7 L-R 2c, jeehyun 16 T-B 5, Ajintai 121 6b, Hibrida 18b, 18b, 18b, Ksenya Savva 68c, 9 L-R 1b, 120 R T-B 3, Chareez 32c, Apichat Khutchita 121 3b, kzww 70t, Dmitry Kalinovsky 88 R T-B 4, cigdem 142 L-R 4t, Olivier Le Moal 52b, voronas 77 L-R 4b, Abramova Elena 8 L-R 3t, iurii 142c, thananya 47, operative401 121 7b, Sergio Schnitzler 90 T-B 2, SaveJungle 39c, Smirnova Galina 120 R T-B 1, Alexis kapsaskis 26 L-R 6t, Slaval7 100 L-R 3c, sagir 90 T-B 5, Olga_Shestakova 100 L-R 1c, domnitsky 77 L-R 5b, Sanit Fuangnakhon 98 T-B 1, Bogdan ionescu 118 L-R 5t, Nina Fedorova 58 R T-B 3, 58 R T-B 4, Aldona Griskeviciene 65 L-R 1b, 65 L-R 2b, Africa Studio 99c, 124 2 L-R 4c, Kibri_ho 89b, irin-k 24 L-R 2t, Pack 7 L-R 1b, 7 L-R 1c, 7 L-R 2b, John Kasawa 12 L-R 3t, fivespots 71c, Stepan Bormotov 84 L-R 1t, Eduard Radu 58 R T-B 5, Igor Drondin 116 L-R 4t, ivandivandelen 73c, MaraZe 14c, Fotos593 46 R T-B 1, Svetlana Serebryakova 124 1 L-R 2t, gresei 10 L-R 2t, Studio_G 104c, 105c, Ivengo 120 R T-B 2, vipman 8 L-R 4t, Incredible Arctic 46 R T-B 2, Krivosheev Vitaly 110 L T-B 2, 124 1

L-R 3t, Tsekhmister 46 L T-B 2, gillmar 24 L-R 3t, artist-ka 27 L-R 1t, Elena Schweitzer 116 L-R 2t, Rosa Jay 46 L T-B 5, SERASOOT 44c, Butterfly Hunter 77 L-R 1b, Photoonlife 124 1 L-R 1t, CloudyStock 18 T-B 3b, Andrii_M 58 R T-B 2, Aliaksei Design 98 T-B 5, Richard Griffin 94c, Altagracia Art 14c, 14c, 14c, Robyn Mackenzie 8 L-R 2t, Susanto Anto 9 L-R 2t, Oleg Nesterov 100t, frantic00 31c, Purino 20 L T-B 1, miha de 82c, nexus 7 16 T-B 1, Tartila 98 T-B 4, Nerthuz 124 2 L-R 2c, Nevada31 134, Phive 142 L-R 1t, Sashkin 118 L-R 1t, Coloringbook 120 L T-B 1, Pete Pahham 114 L-R 1t, dslaven 116 L-R 1t, wizdata 24c, Azure_Sun 9 L-R 1t, Olga Guchek 12 L-R 1t, Vasyl Hubar 77 L-R 3b, RG-vc 88 R T-B 3.